# Xi Jinping's China

# XI JINPING'S CHINA

## The Personal and the Political

Stig Stenslie and
Marte Kjær Galtung

LYNNE
RIENNER
PUBLISHERS

BOULDER
LONDON

*An earlier version of this book was published in Norwegian
in 2022 by Universitetsforlaget.*

Paperback edition published in the United States of America in 2025 by
Lynne Rienner Publishers, Inc.
1800 30th Street, Suite 314, Boulder, Colorado 80301
www.rienner.com

ISBN: 978-1-962551-37-3 (pb: alk. paper)

**Library of Congress Cataloging-in-Publication Data**
A Cataloging-in-Publication record for the hardcover edition of
this book is available from the Library of Congress.

**British Cataloguing in Publication Data**
A Cataloguing in Publication record for the hardcover edition of
this book is available from the British Library.

Printed and bound in the United States of America

The paper used in this publication meets the requirements
of the American National Standard for Permanence of
Paper for Printed Library Materials Z39.48-1992.

5   4   3   2   1

# Contents

# Acknowledgments

WE STARTED STUDYING CHINESE POLITICS TOGETHER IN 2008, ONE year after the Chinese Communist Party Congress, which takes place every five years. Xi Jinping had then been elected to the Politburo's Standing Committee, making him one of the handful of men constituting the supreme leadership of the country and eventually its paramount leader at the next congress in 2012. Events leading up to this 2012 congress were to prove highly dramatic. Bo Xilai—China's biggest political celebrity and a candidate for one of the top posts— fell out of favor in the greatest political earthquake since the student uprising in 1989, sending tremors all the way to our offices in Oslo. Xi was pretty much a blank page to us when he became general secretary of the Chinese Communist Party in 2012. In addition, China was a quite different country then.

During his first decade in power, Xi has unleashed China as a superpower on the world stage and clearly challenged the United States. At the same time, he has steered the country toward a much more authoritarian regime. With his renomination as the general secretary of the Chinese Communist Party in October 2022, Xi seems to have set the course to rule China indefinitely. This makes him the key to understanding the rising superpower.

Most rewarding as we worked on this book were our many discussions with friends and colleagues in Norway and abroad. As part of a continual learning process, these conversations helped us to better understand the development of Xi's China. Several people made suggestions and commented on the text. In particular, we would like to mention Bjørn Elias Mikaelsen Grønning, Trygve Gulbrandsen, Sun Haifeng, Henrik Ståhane Hiim, Henning Kristoffersen, Kjersti Litleskare, Siv Helland Oftedal, Rune Svarverud, and Bjørnar Sverdrup-Thygeson. Thanks also go to Lynne Rienner Publishers, especially to our excellent editor, Marie-Claire Antoine, for her belief in the project, support, and cooperation throughout the writing process, and to John Meyrick for translating the book from Norwegian to English.

Last but not least, we thank our spouses, Steve and Amber, for their patience, and our children, Ask, Isak, and little Nora, who had to spend their first years with Xi Dada.

# 1

# Leadership and Politics in China

TWO TRAITS CHARACTERIZE XI JINPING'S FIRST DECADE IN OFFICE. First, he has unleashed the tiger; under his leadership, China has demonstrated a will and an ability to challenge the United States as the dominant superpower. Second, and in parallel with this development, there has been a considerable concentration of power within China, leading many observers to claim that Xi is the country's strongest leader since Mao Zedong, who founded the People's Republic of China (PRC) in 1949. Some even contend that he is more powerful than Mao.[1] What is certain is that Xi Jinping's China is far more powerful than Mao's. Because of his position and China's new role as a superpower in the international arena, Xi was featured as "the world's most powerful man" on the cover of *The Economist*.[2] His ambitions and visions, not to mention his will and ability to push through his policies, are what shape China. Xi is the key to understanding this new superpower.

Like Mao, Xi was born in the Year of the Snake. In Chinese tradition, each year in a twelve-year cycle belongs to an animal: rat, ox, tiger, hare, dragon, snake, horse, sheep, monkey, rooster, dog, and pig. Those born in the Year of the Snake are said to be charming, positive, and enterprising. They can be dangerous, however, so you would not want someone born in the Year of the Snake as your enemy. They tend to run their own race and can be headstrong and authoritarian.

1

They are also tough. Most of all, those born in the Year of the Snake are often thirsty for power and will do anything to quench this thirst.[3]

## The Supreme Leader

In the West, China's supreme leader is often referred to as its "president." This is misleading, as such a title underplays the leader's real power.

China's political system consists of three main components: the Communist Party, the government, and the military. In this system, the government and the military are subordinate to the party—even more so in Xi Jinping's China than in previous decades. The leader of the PRC is first and foremost the general secretary of the Communist Party of China (see Figure 1.1), the undisputed top position of the power pyramid. The leader also holds the title of president (see Figure 1.2) of the government and head of the military. It is in the highest party bodies—such as the Politburo and its Standing Committee, as well as the Central Committee—that the national political agenda is set and important decisions are made. The government and the military must obediently implement these decisions.

The general secretary has control over a party apparatus of about 96 million members and, through it, control over: the world's most populous state (with 1.4 billion people); the world's largest standing armed force (roughly 2 million); and an economy set to become the world's biggest. In addition, the party has absolute control over the legislative and judicial powers, the media, public opinion, and education. The United States is still militarily stronger and far richer than China as measured in gross national product per inhabitant, but the US separation-of-powers model means that the power of the office of the president is greatly limited compared to that of the Chinese general secretary.

### The Legacies of Mao Zedong and Deng Xiaoping

The country's leaders have undoubtedly all left their mark on China, and the PRC's early history is synonymous with the history of Mao Zedong and Deng Xiaoping.

Figure 1.1   Leadership Organization Within the Chinese Communist Party

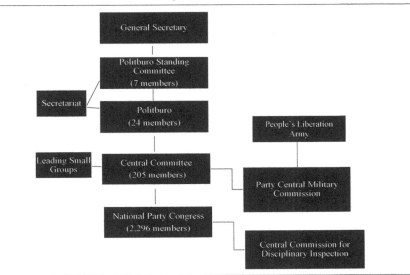

*Source:* "China's 2017 Communist Party Leadership Structure & Transition," US-China Business Council. June 2017, p. 2. https://www.uschina.org/sites/default /files/LeadershipReport.pdf.
*Note:* Chinese Communist Party groups are in shaded boxes.

It was Mao who led the Communists to victory against outer and inner enemies: the Japanese, who occupied large parts of China before and during World War II, and the Chinese Nationalist Party (Guomindang) under the leadership of Chiang Kai-shek, who fled to Taiwan after his defeat. On October 1, 1949, Mao proclaimed the new People's Republic of China from a podium above the Gate of Heavenly Peace, the main entrance to the Forbidden City, from which the emperors had reigned. Now it was the Communists who would "rule over everything under the heavens." These deeds secured an unrivaled position for Mao both within the party and among the Chinese people. He had united the country and rebuilt the people's self-respect in the wake of what the Chinese call the "century of humiliation," which began when the First Opium War (1839–1842) initiated an era of foreign invasion, civil war, and unimaginable suffering for the Chinese people.

Figure 1.2  Government of the People's Republic of China

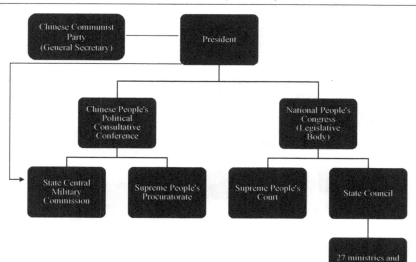

*Source:* "China's 2017 Communist Party Leadership Structure & Transition," US-China Business Council. June 2017, p. 2. https://www.uschina.org/sites/default /files/LeadershipReport.pdf.

Mao used his power to transform Chinese society and economy after the Soviet model, launching, among other things, a large-scale program for industrialization and agricultural collectivization. The Chinese people were to pay a heavy price, however. Meant to turn China into an industrial and military great power, the Great Leap Forward (1958–1961) inflicted even more suffering and death. This was followed by the Cultural Revolution (1966–1976), which reduced the country to chaos and was launched because Mao, who felt that his position had been weakened both within the party and among the people, attempted to restore his standing and power by putting into practice his theory of "permanent revolution." The result was anarchy, during which the Red Guards wreaked havoc on traditions and culture to achieve a Communist nirvana. Estimates of how many died directly or indirectly because of Mao's policies range from 40 million to 70 million.[4]

Mao's successor, Deng Xiaoping, charted a new course for China when he came to power in 1978. While Mao was described as a populistic tyrant, one who mobilized the masses to hold onto his absolute power, Deng was seen as a pragmatist—someone concerned with practical results. Deng shifted the focus from ideology and mass mobilization to economic growth, as illustrated by two of his best known and most significant political slogans.[5] The first, "Let some become rich first," meant that economic growth was now more important than the purely Marxist aim of economic equality.[6] The second, "It does not matter whether the cat is black or white, if the cat can catch mice, it is a good cat," reflected a change from an ideological to a more pragmatic approach to politics and social development.[7] During Deng's term, the Chinese economy transformed from a closed, planned economy to a market economy with far greater contact with the rest of the world, a period the Chinese refer to as "reform and opening."

Deng also made important reforms to the system of government to prevent power from landing again in the hands of an omnipotent ruler such as Mao. In 1982, he set a limit of two five-year terms for top leaders, laying the foundations for a functioning system of leadership change, the Achilles' heel of any authoritarian regime. Moreover, he took another step to avoid a future omnipotent leader by introducing collective leadership at the top of the party, which meant that members of the Politburo's Standing Committee would now enjoy a considerable degree of autonomy and could make decisions collectively on important matters. Despite these reforms, Deng did not shy away from ensuring the party's survival. Ultimately, he was the one who gave the order to crush the students' protests at Tiananmen Square in 1989—and with it hopes for democracy in China at the time.

The thoughts and decisions of Mao and Deng shaped the lives of generations of Chinese for better or worse. But leadership has its limitations. As Karl Marx remarked, "Men make their own history, but they do not make it as they will. They do not make it under circumstances chosen by themselves, but under circumstances directly found, created, and passed on by the past."[8] Despite the considerable powers of the general secretary of the Chinese Communist Party, not all leaders have been as strong as Mao and Deng. Hu Jintao, Xi's immediate predecessor, who ruled from 2002 to 2012, was far weaker than both Mao and Deng. He was a technocrat and party man above all, and his power as party leader was hampered by a number of factors, including his personality, his ambitions, and the strength of other party leaders. Within the Communist Party, Hu's term was spoken of as "the lost decade," a decade of lost opportunities, while Western observers asked sarcastically, "Who's Hu?"

In contrast, Xi Jinping is without doubt an extraordinarily strong leader, a modern Chinese emperor.[9] *Xi's Thoughts* are now included in the constitutions of both the party and the state, and the law has been changed so that, in principle, he can remain in power for the rest of his life. Moreover, a personality cult has developed around Xi, the like of which has not been seen since Mao.

## Xi Jinping's Path

Xi is four years younger than the People's Republic of China, and his life and road to power mirror the PRC's history. He was born in 1953 into the power elite as the son of Mao's vice premier, Xi Zhongxun. His father was a hero of the Communist revolution who had helped Mao rise to power. Xi's family lived in safe and sheltered, but not extravagant, circumstances, a privileged existence that would come to a brutal end four years before the Cultural Revolution, when his father was expelled as a counterrevolutionary. Xi's family was humiliated during Mao's brutal campaign. Like so many urban youths, Xi was sent to the countryside to be "reeducated," an overwhelming experience for him and a whole generation of Chinese. Toward the end of the Cultural Revolution, things changed for the better, and Xi was eventually allowed into the Communist Party.

Xi started his political career in the early 1980s, at the same time that Deng Xiaoping opened China's economy. At first, the east coast particularly benefitted from the market reforms, which laid the foundations for several decades of amazing growth, and it was in the coastal provinces of Fujian and Zhejiang that Xi held his first important political posts. In 2007, Xi was brought back to Beijing as a member of the Politburo's Standing Committee. He had reached the top echelon of the party and was well positioned to take over power in the nascent superpower five years later.

In 2012, many China observers thought Xi would turn out to be a weak leader. The Hong Kong–based journalist and writer Willy Wo-Lap Lam believed Xi would be the weakest Chinese leader for several decades because he had come to power in the wake of the divisive political scandals that led up to the eighteenth party congress, leaving the party weakened by power struggles and stripped of popular support. An important political event that draws the attention of experts on China, known as "China Hands," the National Congress of the Chinese Communist Party, or simply the party congress, is in theory China's highest political body or institution. Since the death of Mao Zedong, the congress has been held predictably every five autumns, gathering party delegates from all over China for one week in the Great Hall of the People in the heart of Beijing. Overarching ideological guidelines and leadership roles for the coming term are established during the congress, most importantly those of the Politburo and the Politburo's Standing Committee.

Some also expected that Xi would be weak because the Politburo was dominated by people appointed by his predecessors (Jiang Zemin and Hu Jintao) and Xi lacked a power base within the party.[10] Sinologist Cheng Li from the Brookings Institution in Washington wrote, "At the start of their tenure, the upcoming generation of leaders, led by the dual-successor pair Xi Jinping and Li Keqiang, are likely even weaker than their predecessors due to their lack of previous achievements, their need to share power and the growing competitive pressure among their peers."[11]

As for Xi's political orientation, several took him to be a "reformist" who would weaken the party state's control over the economy in favor of private businesses. Nicholas Kristof, a *New York Times* journalist, remarked that Xi's father had been among the more liberal advisors to Deng Xiaoping, the man who opened the Chinese economy, and therefore reform was in Xi's genes.[12] Kristof suggested that Xi would even permit a certain opening in politics.

It was also a common perception that because of Xi's personal experiences under Mao's regime of terror, he more than anyone understood the dangers of despotism.

Xi would prove that these predictions were well off the mark.

## Understanding Chinese Leadership and Politics

Given the regime's closed character, understanding politics in China is a baffling activity.[13] Access to reliable information about what goes on inside Zhongnanhai, Beijing's equivalent to the Kremlin, where Xi and the other members of the top political elite live, is highly limited. This fires up rumors and speculation among diplomats stationed in China, journalists in Hong Kong, and Chinese dissidents in exile. But almost all stories about what is going on are pure fantasy. As the Chinese philosopher Laozi observed as early as 600 BC, "Those who talk, do not know; those who know, do not talk."[14] Furthermore, Western observers tend to read Chinese politics through their own normative spectacles, and many of the predictions that were put forward when Xi came to power would appear to be wishful thinking ten years later.

"Beijingology," the study of politics in China, has, if anything, become even more difficult under Xi, who by nature is cautious and hides his true intentions. Many who have previously worked with Xi will say that these are his dominant personality traits.[15] Almost a decade into Xi Jinping's tenure, China expert Jeffrey Wasserstrom raised the question of why there is not a single good biography of China's leader.[16] On the shelves of bookshops you can find biographies of other leaders, such as Russia's Vladimir Putin, the Philippines' Rodrigo Duterte, Hungary's Viktor Orbán, and North Korea's Kim Jong-un, but you will be hard-pressed to find one decent biography of Xi Jinping.[17] This is strange, given that Xi has been China's strongest leader for several decades and is arguably one of the world's most powerful men. But few, if any, who know him will talk about him. Maybe this is out of loyalty as much as out of fear of reprisals, should they fall into disfavor with the leader. Xi keeps his cards close to his chest. If you stand outside his inner circle, it is virtually impossible to gain access to him. He rarely gives interviews, never takes questions after his speeches, and tightly controls the narrative and presentation of his and China's history. Previous Chinese leaders were more open; Jiang Zemin, who led the PRC between 1989 and 2002, gave an interview to *60 Minutes*, a US news broadcast. There are few biographies of Hu Jintao, not because he was impossible to get ahold of, but because, according to Wasserstrom, he was too boring a character to be the subject of a book. Xi, however, is far from boring. He is just inaccessible.[18]

Despite the difficulty of studying politics in China under Xi Jinping, and the enigmatic nature of Xi himself, it is more important than ever to put the pieces of available information together to understand the man who has so much say for the development of China and, thereby, the world. There is a gap to bridge between the "art" and "science" of reading Chinese elite politics, or between traditional Beijingology and purely academically relevant research. On the far "art" end of the spectrum, one finds the rumor mill among Beijing diplomats and, until recently, the speculations in the Hong Kong press.[19] Among methodological pitfalls are the risks of reading too much into minute changes in newspaper vocabularies or becoming carried away with reading tea leaves and listening to rumors about intraparty strife, which the larger picture of relative stability in the Chinese political elite passes over.[20] Along the outer reaches of the "science" end of the spectrum, quantitative elite studies are systematic and analytically stringent, but they often share the weaknesses common to quantitative studies: either being based on general theories of social science too disconnected from the specific political realities of China, or providing answers to questions too long-term or too theoretical in nature to be of immediate relevance to those seeking to divine the political decisionmaking in Zhongnanhai. While China Hands tend to focus too narrowly on China as an idiosyncratic case, quantitatively oriented social scientists tend to focus too broadly to fully account for the specificities of the Chinese political system. In short, there is a pressing need for a new Beijingology, combining the traditional art of China watching with the most innovative methods and tools derived from social science research into elite studies and textual analyses.[21]

## About the Book

This book is not meant to be a biography of Xi but rather of the contemporary history of China. We make use of Xi to investigate today's China, looking for answers to several vital questions: Who is Xi Jinping? Why and how did he and not someone else rise to the top as the Chinese Communist Party's general secretary and the president of China? How did he become such a dominating leader? Why has a personality cult developed around him, and how is this perceived by the Chinese? What is his political project for China and his vision for China in the world? And, the inevitable comparison, is Xi a new Mao?

We begin to address these questions in Chapter 2, "Xi's Climb Through the Ranks," which examines how and why Xi rose to become the most powerful man in China. Xi started his political career at the bottom of the organizational hierarchy that is the Communist Party of China and showed his political and managerial skills while climbing the ranks. He was, however, far from alone in doing this. We argue that his personal traits and survival skills, flexibility, ambitiousness, and keen understanding of when to openly take sides on controversial issues were among the decisive factors in securing his success in reaching the top of the party.

Chapter 3, "Concentrating Power," explores how Xi secured for himself an all-powerful position not seen in China since Deng, or perhaps even Mao. We ask whether this power concentration under Xi has been a collective answer to governance challenges or a result of his personal hunger for power. This is an important question to raise, as the answer is key to understanding the dynamics at the top of the political system and whether they are marked by despotism, power struggles, and fear, or by more open debates about the challenges facing the Communist Party, consensus around the rules of political games, and cooperation among key political leaders and networks.

Chapter 4, "Extolling the Leader," discusses the cult of personality that has risen around Xi. The party elite, assessing that a strong leader is essential in handling the problems facing China and maintaining the legitimacy of the Communist Party, have arguably permitted and encouraged a personal focus and worship of Xi paralleled only by Mao and the leaders of North Korea. Importantly, the chapter explores the limits to which a cult of personality can be pushed before the cult loses all credibility and looks for signs that it has gone too far and backfires on Xi and the party.

Chapter 5, "An Ideological Renaissance," dives into Xi's political agenda. All predictions of Xi as a reform-oriented market liberalist who would initiate an opening up in China, economically as well as politically, proved wrong. Rather, Xi has reversed the political trends of pragmatism and watering down ideology, which have characterized Chinese society and politics since Deng. Marxist ideology and indeed Mao himself are undergoing a renaissance in politics as well as in society in general.

Chapter 6, "Stepping onto the World Stage," turns the focus outward to Xi's impact on China's relations with the world. China's foreign policy from the 1980s to the 2000s was guided by Deng's mantra of "laying low and hiding one's capabilities," prioritizing domestic development over international influence. Under Xi, Beijing has bid a final farewell to the cautiousness of the last thirty years. China has come out as a great power state and demands to be treated as such. More than anything, this is visible in China's diplomatic corps, labeled the "wolf warriors," unconventional, uncompromising, offensive, assertive, and undiplomatic as they are. However, the new style has engendered backlash, as other countries find common ground in their anxieties over China and take steps to handle, and even prevent, its further rise.

Finally, Chapter 7 concludes the book and takes as its point of departure the conspicuous similarities between Xi and Mao. Xi resembles the old chairman with his charisma, dominant role within the party, and hard line toward political opponents. The cult of personality around Xi is also a blast from the past, bringing up the question, "Is Xi a new Mao?"

\*    \*    \*

Throughout the book, we make a point of introducing the reader to some key words, expressions, and proper nouns that occur in modern Chinese. We have tried to be consistent in our use of the Pinyin system.

For instance, this means we write "Mao Zedong" instead of "Mao Tse-tung," "Beijing" instead of "Peking," and "Guomindang" instead of "Kuomintang," which were standard under the Wades-Giles system. We have left out indication of tones.

However, we made exceptions for some proper nouns. This is the case when there are already well-established spellings in English so that a Pinyin transcription would only confuse the reader. We do not, therefore, correct the spellings of Sun Tzu, Mencius, Chiang Kaishek, Taoism, Tsinghua University, or Peking University. For the same reason, for some Chinese scholars who are well known outside China, we have used the Western ordering of their names rather than the correct Chinese order. We refer to Li Cheng as Cheng Li and Pei Minxin as Minxin Pei.

## Notes

1. Andrew J. Nathan, "Who Is Xi," *New York Review of Books*, May 12, 2016, www.nybooks.com/articles/2016/05/12/who-is-xi.

2. "The World's Most Powerful Man: Xi Jinping Has More Clout Than Donald Trump: The World Should Be Wary," *The Economist*, October 14, 2017.

3. Sun Heidi Sæbu, *Kina—den nye supermakten: Jakten på Xi Jinping og det moderne Kina* [China—the new superpower: the hunt for Xi Jinping and modern China] (Oslo: Kagge, 2019), 292.

4. Jonathan Fenby, *The Penguin History of Modern China: The Fall and Rise of a Great Power, 1850–2008* (London: Allen Lane, 2008), 351.

5. Barry Naughton, "Deng Xiaoping: The Economist," *China Quarterly* 135 (1993): 491–514.

6. "邓小平：让一部分人先富起来" [Deng Xiaoping: let some people get rich first], *Zhongguo Gongchandang xinwen*, http://cpc.people.com.cn/GB /34136/2569304.html.

7. "邓小平同志'黑猫白猫论'背后的故事" [The history behind Comrade Deng Xiaoping's theory of black and white cat], *Zhongguo Gongchandang xinwen*, http://cpc.people. com.cn/GB/85037/8530953.html.

8. Karl Marx, *The Eighteenth Brumaire of Louis Bonaparte* (Mondial, 2015; first published 1852).

9. For the terms used in this chapter to describe the men who ruled the People's Republic of China, see David Shambaugh, *China's Leaders: From Mao to Now* (Cambridge, UK: Polity Press, 2021).

10. Willy Wo-Lap Lam, quoted in "Xi to Be 'Weak' President," *Radio Free Asia*, November 12, 2012, www.rfa.org/english/news/china/xi-jinping-11122012110129.html.

11. Cheng Li, "The End of CCP's Resilient Authoritarianism? A Tripartite Assessment of Shifting Power in China," *China Quarterly* 211 (2012): 595–623. The quotation comes from p. 609.

12. Nicholas Kristof, "Looking for a Jump-Start in China," *New York Times*, January 5, 2013.

13. Several authors have pointed out that understanding of Chinese politics has been flawed ever since the founding of the People's Republic. See, for instance, Frederick C. Teiwes, "The Study of Elite Politics in PRC: Politics Inside the 'Black Box'," in David S. G. Goodman (ed.), *Handbook of Politics of China* (Cheltenham, UK: Edward Elgar, 2015), 21–41.

14. Laozi, 道德經 [Daodejing, or the book about the road and its virtue], verse 62, chapter 56.

15. See, for example, Joseph Torigian, "Historical Legacies and Leaders' Worldviews: Communist Party History and Xi's Learned (and Unlearned) Lessons," *China Perspectives*, June 2018, 11, https://journals.openedition.org/chinaperspectives/7548; Frederick Teiwes in Graeme Smith and Louisa Lim, "Xi Dada and Daddy: Power, the Party and the President," *The Little Red Podcast*, November 2, 2020, https://omny.fm/shows/the-little-red-podcast/xi-dada-and-daddy-power-the-party-and-the-presiden.

16. Jeffrey Wasserstrom, "Why Are There No Biographies of Xi Jinping?" *The Atlantic*, January 30, 2021, www.theatlantic.com/international/archive/2021/01/xi-jinping-china-biography/617852.

17. Two recently published exceptions are Stefan Aust and Adrian Geiges, *Xi Jinping: The Most Powerful Man in the World* (Cambridge, UK: Polity, 2022); Alfred Chan, *Xi Jinping: Political Career, Governance, and Leadership, 1953–2018* (Oxford: Oxford University Press, 2022).

18. Wasserstrom, "Why Are There No Biographies of Xi Jinping?"

19. Andrei Lungu, "China's Next President: Reading the Tea Leaves of Chinese Politics," *The Diplomat*, September 29, 2017.

20. M. Yahuda, "Kremlinology and the Chinese Strategic Debate, 1965–66," *China Quarterly* 49 (1972): 33–36.

21. Bjørnar Sverdrup Thygeson and Stig Stenslie, "Beijingology 2.0: Bridging the 'Art' and 'science' of China Watching in Xi Jinping's New Era," *International Journal of Intelligence and CounterIntelligence*, July 18, 2022.

# 2

# Xi's Climb
# Through the Ranks

THE CLIMB TO THE TOP HAS BEEN LONG FOR XI JINPING, AS HE started at the bottom. The first leader to be born after the founding of the People's Republic, he is also the first to belong to the generation whose youth was affected by the dramatic Cultural Revolution. He joined the Communist Party at twenty-one and soon became the leader of a village committee. From there he rapidly climbed up the party hierarchy, rising to top posts, first as the head of cities and provinces and ultimately to the very highest as general secretary. At each stage, he proved himself skilled, delivered results, and was found worthy of promotion to the next level. Xi was far from being the only one to deliver good results, however, for there were lots of rivals in the enormous party apparatus with its tens of millions of members.

An outstanding feature of Xi is his ability to survive. First, he survived the trauma of Mao Zedong's Cultural Revolution when he was sent from a sheltered and safe existence in the capital to forced labor in the countryside. Xi also survived the next political earthquake brought on by the market reforms and opening of the economy that Deng Xiaoping initiated in the 1980s. For Chinese politicians and officials at all levels, this created an ocean of possibilities for lavish personal enrichment. Many a career crashed because of greed. As far as we can judge, Xi managed to resist the temptations that must have lured him wherever he turned, for he has never been involved in any corruption scandal.

Throughout his career, Xi has proved himself an ambitious and purposeful politician. In hindsight, it is easy to see personal ambition reflected in all the life and career choices he has made since his youth. Soon after university he left a secure job in Beijing for a post at the lowest level in the countryside, which shows that even then he had political ambitions. On his way to the top, however, he was careful to hide them, while in a discreet and innocuous manner ensuring that the right people were aware of his achievements. Xi learned early on the value of holding his cards close to his chest. As a little boy, he witnessed the punishment meted out to his father, vice premier under Mao, for daring to speak out against Mao.

Yet at all times Xi has shown determination and great political flair and managed the difficult balance of hiding his personal ambitions and getting noticed.

## From Privileged Princeling to Cave-Dweller

The Great Proletarian Cultural Revolution started in 1966. Mao's wife, Jiang Qing, was given the mission of shaping a new cultural policy for the People's Liberation Army (PLA). It brought a decade of chaos, turmoil, and terror. Mao started it all as a means of restoring his power, which he felt was being threatened. After all the suffering and problems the Great Leap Forward (1958–1961) brought, many top leaders viewed Mao with skepticism.

Mao's goal had been to transform China into an economic, technological, and military great power. The road to success, Mao believed, was the mobilization of the energy of the masses. Mao gave priority to the countryside, which was collectivized to increase production. The peasants had to work on great collective projects instead of in their own fields, which in many cases were left to lie fallow. Famine followed. Another target was steel production. Once more it was up to the masses. Starting in the autumn of 1958, 90 million people were set to produce steel. They dutifully collected all kinds of metal and smelted it regardless of whether it was suitable or not. Poor people often sacrificed the kitchen utensils they needed in their households to primitive backyard furnaces that produced worthless material.

The consequences were disastrous: between 20 million and 45 million died, mostly of hunger.[1]

Mao feared he would be judged after his death, like Joseph Stalin in 1953, or deposed before his death, like Nikita Khrushchev in 1964. This is why he wanted to break down the existing party bureaucracy, which he felt threatened his position.[2] Mao urged the masses to wage a continual revolution. Under the motto "No construction without destruction"[3] (不破不立)—or "You can't make an omelet without breaking eggs"—the revolution spread quickly from the cultural sector to the political, social, economic, and educational sectors. The Chinese political system was first thrown into chaos, then paralyzed.[4]

Mao ordered the destruction of everything that was old—customs, habits, culture, thoughts. These categories were left undefined, so it was up to all the Red Guards, Mao's paramilitary student groups, to decide which institutions and individuals fell into these categories. Everything and everyone who someone or another felt belonged to the old could be attacked, including party leaders at various levels. Anarchy ruled. Various radical groups with no central leadership fought those in power at all levels—and each other. Who had power in a particular place and whom it was safe to be on good terms with could change from day to day. The mood in Chinese society was a mixture of euphoria, fear, confusion, and tension, described by Roderick MacFarquhar and Michael Schoenhals as "volcanic energy."[5]

Most educational institutions were closed because they were regarded as transmitters of the old that one now wanted to smash. As a result, a whole generation of Chinese received little or no education.

During the Cultural Revolution, several million were persecuted, accused of being right-wing, bourgeois, and capitalist. They were exposed to humiliation, imprisonment, torture, and execution. Many committed suicide to escape the suffering. About 17 million were sent to the countryside to be reeducated and purified through forced labor.[6] Estimates of the number of unnatural deaths during the Cultural Revolution range from several hundred thousand to several millions.[7]

Until the Cultural Revolution, Xi and his family had lived a privileged life in Beijing because of Xi's father's position in the party. His father had been a guerrilla fighter who had helped liberate China from its occupiers, unite the country, and establish the People's Republic. At the time he was vice premier, while Xi's mother worked at the Central Party School. They lived in a big house with Xi and his three siblings, along with a cook, a guard, and a maid. They had access to health services, and Xi attended kindergarten in the beautiful Beihai Park. Both parents were often absent from home. His father worked long days as vice premier, and his mother worked so far away that she was home only during the weekends. His father was strict, even by Chinese standards of the day, and the little time he had with the children in the evenings he spent teaching them Confucian morals.[8]

During the Cultural Revolution, Xi's family were among those attacked and mistreated. By 1962, four years prior to the Cultural Revolution, Xi's father had lost all his political posts after being accused on the thinnest of grounds of supporting a novelist regarded as critical of Mao. Fair game for Mao's Red Guards, he was humiliated and beaten during public "struggle sessions" or "self-criticism meetings." During such sessions those who had committed political errors, more or less serious, were both criticized and given a chance for self-criticism. The struggles that took place during such meetings were verbal to begin with but often degenerated into extreme violence. The aim was supposedly to give the accused self-insight so that they might realize they were on the wrong side in the ongoing class struggle and be rehabilitated, but most ended up being purged. Xi, his siblings, and his mother had to attend these meetings. Xi's mother was pressured into publicly denouncing her own husband. His father was first put under house arrest and then imprisoned, while his mother was sent to a labor camp.[9] The humiliation and violence must have made a strong impression on Xi, who at the start of the Cultural Revolution was a young boy of thirteen. His half sister is said to have been so traumatized by the persecution and brutality she and her family experienced that she took her own life.[10]

Without his father's protection, the fifteen-year-old Xi was sent from Beijing to forced labor at Yan'an in Shaanxi Province. We have little insight into Xi's life during the first two years of the Cultural Revolution, and the circumstances around his ending up in the countryside are unclear. Some historians believe he was forced to leave, while others think he volunteered.[11] In any event, he was one of about 17 million city youths and students who were sent to the countryside to work and learn from the peasants.

Mao's view of peasants differed from the traditional Marxist view, in which they have little revolutionary potential. During the struggle with the Nationalists in the 1920s and 1930s, the Communists sought refuge in rural areas, and this contributed to Mao's perception that peasants were closer to the correct ideological line than privileged urbanites were. Therefore, he sent city youths into the countryside en masse, causing a mass migration. All over China columns of youths traipsed along the roads on foot or were crowded into lorries, buses, or trains, singing revolutionary songs. Sent out of the cities, they were met by welcoming committees in the villages.

Life was definitely different and much tougher for Xi and the other townees. Xi is said to have been badly treated by the villagers who, because of his father, told him he deserved to be shot a hundred times. Plus, he was not used to physical labor. After just three months he chose to run away to Beijing. He was soon caught, and after six months of detention, he was released on condition that he returned. It is hard to know whether it is true that his uncle and aunt persuaded him to do so. They supposedly confronted him with the following ultimatum: either you end up like your father, humiliated and alone in jail, or your mother, in forced labor, or your sister, who has taken her own life, or you go back to the countryside and make the best of it by being a model student-worker. Xi eventually saw the light and chose the last option. This time he went to the village of Liangjiahe, also in Shaanxi Province, where he spent the last six years of the Cultural Revolution. There Xi senior had a network, so the local cadres protected young Xi, and he was better treated by the local peasants.[12]

These seven long years in the countryside had a big effect on Xi in several ways. Several of his most important friendships date back to this period. There he met the present vice president, Wang Qishan, who came to be one of Xi's most trusted friends and remains so today. They lived in the same dugout cave and shared a bed, and Wang gave Xi books on economics. They remained in touch, and Xi has since given Wang responsibility for several areas of decisive importance to him. As leader of the Central Commission for Disciplinary Inspection from 2012 to 2017, Wang was responsible for the anticorruption campaign, one of Xi's prestige projects, which set its stamp upon the first five-year period of his government.

This involuntary stay in the countryside gave him personal experience and invaluable knowledge of conditions among the poor peasants of China. Xi has strategically used this to build his reputation and legitimacy both on his road to the top and while there. He claims that his roots as a civil servant are in northern, upland Shaanxi, a place where he gained a lasting conviction. Xi writes, "Do something good for the people! Wherever I go, I will always be a son of the Loess Plateau."[13] By expressing himself in this way, Xi links himself both to the heart of China and to proud parts of its history. The Loess Plateau, often called "the yellow soil," is reckoned to be the cradle of Chinese civilization. By declaring himself the son of the yellow soil, Xi underlines his direct bond both to China's rich history through the legendary yellow emperor and to the Communist Party's base before the revolution of 1949.[14] To mark this bond he has visited the village he lived in several times.[15]

An example of how he describes the insight he gained during this period is a speech he held on a visit to the United States in 2015: "The villagers and I lived in 'earth caves' and slept on 'earth beds.' Life was very hard. There was no meat in our diet for months. I knew what the villagers wanted the most. Later I became the village's party secretary and began to lead the villagers in production. I understood their needs."[16] For his public at home, he described his experiences in this way: "My rural assignment was a landmark moment in my life. It redirected and purified me, a rebirth for me. If I have gained any true knowledge, any maturity or success, or any familiarity with the real lives of ordinary people, I acquired all of this from that place."[17]

Here Xi distinguishes himself from his immediate predecessor, Hu Jintao, who has never mentioned his private life with a single word. The official version is that Xi succeeded in his new life in the country and that the local villagers admired him, but there is little we can know with any certainty about Xi's life in this period.

We do, however, know a lot about the experiences of others in the same situation through the considerable amount of what is known in Chinese as "scar literature" (伤痕文学), and it is reasonable to assume that Xi's experiences resemble in many ways those of other young Chinese sent to the countryside to do forced labor. Those who did not have ambitions to become China's leader describe far tougher conditions than Xi has done officially. The accounts make clear that most had a hard time coping with the physical exhaustion, neglect, and feelings of not belonging.

For many, mistreatment and bullying were a part of everyday life for those sent to the countryside as well as those who remained in the cities, as described by language professor Ji Xianli, who was persecuted during the Cultural Revolution because of his high academic post:

> Before I knew what was happening, a series of blows rained down on my head. I could tell that Zhang's weapon of choice was a bicycle chain wrapped in rubber. There was a ringing sound in my ears, and I seemed to see stars, but I stood there rigidly without flinching, not daring to move. My eyes, mouth and nose were burning with pain. I willed myself not to faint. I was so disorientated that I could barely hear Zhang screaming at me. . . . I was barely conscious when I finally heard the command: "Get lost!" Realizing that the wrathful God was being merciful to me again, I hurried back to my room with my tail between my legs.[18]

Margaret Chu, who was persecuted during the Cultural Revolution for her Catholic faith, writes,

> I was dragged to the office. Without any investigation, the officer assembled the entire camp to start a "struggle session" against me. In the session, the officer suddenly asked me whether I had committed my alleged original crime leading to my 8 year sentence. . . . I replied firmly: "I did not commit any crimes." Immediately, two people jumped on me and cut off half of my hair. The officer again asked: "Are you guilty?" I firmly replied: "No." Two people then used a rope to tie my hands backwards tightly. It was connected to a loop around my shoulder and underneath my armpits. It was knotted in

such a way that a slight movement of my hands would cause intense pain. . . . The struggle session lasted for two hours. Afterwards, they untied me and handcuffed me instead. The handcuffs became a part of me for the next one hundred days and nights.[19]

Xi was persecuted from age nine to twenty-one, longer than most other children of the party elite. His childhood and his first years as an adult, his formative years, were to a large extent marked by great uncertainty and chaos. Unlike Donald Trump, Xi has no psychologist niece who can analyze how his childhood has affected how he functions as one of the world's most powerful people, and we, who do not know him, therefore have limited insight into his psyche. All the same, there is reason to think that some of the traits we notice in Xi as a politician stem from the dramatic experiences of his younger years. For instance, he comes across as very unyielding and strong-willed both personally and as head of state.[20] He himself describes how he was toughened up during those hard times in the countryside: "With that kind of experience, whatever difficulties I would encounter in the future, I am fully charged with courage to take on any challenge, to believe in the impossible and to conquer obstacles without panic."[21]

Even if we cannot see inside Xi's head, he comes across as a true believer in the decisive importance of the Communist Party for the development of China. While many of his generation who experienced similar things turned against the party, Xi, on the contrary, seems to be among those who became even more dedicated to it.[22] Probably he thinks that he and his family suffered more *for* than *because of* the party. This makes it even more important to ensure its position of power so that their sufferings will not have been in vain and to ensure his own position within the party to restore the Xi name's honor.[23]

As noted, Xi is known for keeping his cards close to his chest.[24] He has experienced how dangerous it can be to hoist the political flag. After all, the whole family suffered because his father dared to express opinions that did not toe the party line. It is not surprising then that he felt that choosing a career path as a top politician meant avoiding taking sides in controversial issues and avoiding making enemies. Xi comes across both as tough and as a true believer in the

People's Republic and the Communist Party, but he is also known for his flexibility and ability to build compromises.[25]

## Rehabilitation

As the Cultural Revolution approached its end in the mid-1970s, Xi and others who had been blacklisted were gradually rehabilitated. In 1973 he applied for the first time to become a member of the Communist party. His application was refused. Xi did not give up, applied again, and was rejected again. He repeated this nine times in a single year before his tenth application was finally accepted in 1974.[26] Xi had come in from the cold and was speedily appointed village party secretary.[27]

In 1975 he commenced chemical engineering studies at Tsinghua University, Beijing. It is claimed that Xi gained entrance to this prestigious university through a quota system for those sent to do forced labor in villages, because the Cultural Revolution had deprived him, like others who had suffered the same fate, of all opportunity to get an education.[28] Moreover, at this point the universities had been on their knees for a whole decade, so conditions were chaotic when they reopened. Consequently, the quality of the teaching for the first years after the reopening was poorer than both before the closure and later.[29]

After graduating in 1979, Xi got a job in the Central Military Commission as the youngest of three personal secretaries for then defense minister Geng Biao.[30] Such a position gives experience, knowledge, and contacts, which are vital for those who want to advance in the Chinese system. Two years later the Organization Department of the Communist Party is said to have created a section especially for ensuring that the sons and daughters of top party members gained good posts in the party or the government. The whole Xi family was now rehabilitated and selected Xi Jinping as its representative to be taken under the section's wings.[31] He could in earnest begin his career.

At roughly the same time, he married Ke Xiaoming, the daughter of China's ambassador to the United Kingdom. The newlyweds moved into a house owned by her parents. Everything was set for a promising career for Xi in China's military apparatus. It seems to have been a marriage of convenience. The couple quarreled incessantly from the first day, and while Ke wanted to move to London, Xi wanted to stay in China.

## Rising Up Like Feihuang

A poem from the Tang Dynasty (618–907), written to motivate the young to study industriously, tells the story of two boys who, having grown up together, end up in two quite different careers—one at the bottom and one at the top of the social hierarchy. The career of the one at the top is compared to the mythical horse Feihuang's ascent to the heavens. The horse, the successful one, flies so high he can no longer see his friend, the tortoise, down on the ground. When a Chinese person talks of someone "rising up like Feihuang" (飞黄腾达), he is referring to a meteoric rise, as Xi Jinping experienced.

Within a couple of years after having established himself with a job and wife in Beijing, Xi must have decided this was not the career and life he wanted. In 1982 he left his post in the PLA, Beijing, and his unhappy marriage to stake everything on a career in the Communist Party.[32] This was a rougher and more uncertain road, and certainly a big step down, but to begin at the bottom and work his way up was the only way to build a political career. In doing so Xi showed early on his ambitions by moving across the country from one post to another, first in the countryside in Hebei. There he began at the lowest political level—on a village committee. Such committees had relatively little power but were granted a number of unpopular responsibilities, such as collecting taxes and applying the so-called one child policy.[33] As a committee member, Xi gained frontline experience dealing with villagers—a line that must often have seemed more like a firing line. The party's Organization Department noticed that Xi made the rather unusual choice of moving from Beijing to a province three hundred kilometers from the capital—and not just to a province but to a poor agrarian area on the outskirts of the province at that. This contributed to Xi getting noted as "a promising young leader" by the department that had much influence on political appointments.[34]

New challenges and opportunities opened for Xi when Deng Xiaoping became China's leader in 1978, after Mao's death. Deng changed the Communist Party's focus from ideological mobilization to economic growth.[35] In 1979 he launched his idea of special economic zones, areas that would be granted even greater flexibility to carry out market reforms to attract foreign investments. The first cities were Shantou, Shenzhen, and Zhuhai in Guangdong Province, which borders Hong Kong, and Xiamen in Fujian Province opposite Taiwan.[36]

Thus, the east coast was first affected by the economic reforms, and it was here that Xi gained experience while rising through the ranks in various posts. From 1982 to 1985 he held several local party positions in Hebei Province. Hebei surrounds Beijing in the same way that Brandenburg surrounds Berlin so Xi probably had the opportunity to build connections to the central party elite in the capital.

They must have noted him as a promising young leader, for in 1985 he was promoted to deputy mayor of Xiamen, a southern city where much probably seemed foreign to the thirty-two-year-old northerner. In this period Xi reportedly led a simple life, wearing his military uniform from his time in Hebei, taking his meals in the canteen, and laundering his own clothes. Xiamen was one of the special economic zones meant to boost the Chinese economy, so Xi got firsthand experience of the new economic reform policy. He also had much contact with party general secretary Hu Yaobang, who had been a friend and supporter of Xi senior.[37] Xi lost the race for mayor of Xiamen in 1988, instead becoming party secretary, first in the countryside, then in the provincial capital Fuzhou.[38] In this way he gained varied experience.

The Organization Department, the Communist Party's powerful and clandestine human resources department, wants candidates for the party's leading posts to have gained insight and experience from a variety of posts held throughout the country, a plan Xi followed.[39] And he must have convinced the party leadership. In 1997 Xi, now vice governor in Fujian, was a candidate for the party's Central Committee. The committee then had 150 seats. Xi came in at 151.

The number of seats was expanded to 151, probably on the orders of General Secretary Jiang Zemin.[40] At the turn of the millennium, the forty-seven-year-old Xi was promoted to governor of Fujian Province, thereby becoming one of the country's youngest governors.

During his seventeen years in Fujian, Xi was noticed by the party elite, particularly because of the economic growth that occurred under his leadership. When he took over, Fujian lay behind other coastal provinces, but its gross product then rose 13 percent a year, according to official sources.[41] Xi prioritized private business and strong economic growth in line with the prevailing national political trend. He was probably also noticed for being one of few local leaders in Fujian Province not to be involved in a single large-scale corruption scandal at the time.[42] Probably this was largely because he genuinely believed that corruption was harmful for society and the party.[43] That he, unlike many others in the party elite, seems to have avoided exploiting his own political position to help his siblings as business people suggests that he was a genuine opponent of corruption.[44]

Xi had taken a keen interest in ideology already at an early stage, and as governor of Fujian he immersed himself in ideological studies. From 1998 to 2002 he studied Marxist theory at Tsinghua University, obtaining a doctorate in law and ideological education. His thesis was more political than judicial and based on a Marxist understanding of the development stages society goes through; it concluded that the Chinese agricultural sector needed to adjust to the market. Sun Liping, professor of sociology, today one of China's leading intellectuals, was Xi's advisor. Malicious tongues have it that Xi himself wrote little of the thesis and that parts of it are plagiarized, but such claims are hard to confirm or deny.[45]

The same year as he completed his doctorate, Xi's career took yet another quantum leap when he became party secretary, the highest position, in Zhejiang, an important province. In order to modernize the local industry, backward sectors (like textiles and metals) were either downscaled, closed down, or moved out of the province. To replace them he promoted newer, more forward-looking industries, such as information and communication technology and car production.[46] Such a profound restructuring must have met with local opposition, and Xi must have been a forceful leader to overcome it. Zhejiang's economy more than doubled in the five years Xi led the province, from 800 billion RMB in 2002 to 1.9 trillion RMB in 2007.[47] Exports rose 33 percent annually in the same period.[48]

Xi continued to impress the political elite in Beijing, not least through his achievements in the economic field. Even General Secretary Hu Jintao praised Zhejiang when its economy reached 1 trillion RMB. When the post of party secretary in Shanghai became vacant in 2007, Xi was appointed. Having got this far, one began to suspect, Xi could rise all the way to the top.[49] Shanghai, China's biggest city and the country's economic and financial center at the mouth of the mighty Yangtse River, had been the springboard for Jiang Zemin in the 1980s and center for the influential Shanghai clique.

Just as important for Xi's further career as measurable results from Fujian, Zhejiang, and Shanghai was the fact that he kept a low profile and avoided creating enemies. His work style in these posts has been described as "governing by doing nothing."[50] This means not that he was passive or lazy but rather that he avoided confrontations and chose the path of least resistance. Probably this trait comes from his personal knowledge of the cost of taking a stand and landing on the wrong side in political conflicts.

Although Xi was party secretary in Shanghai for only seven months, he succeeded in establishing good relations with the Shanghai clique. In the specialist literature, it is often claimed that at the time the Communist Party consisted of various factions with different backgrounds and political orientations.[51] As the son of one of the founders of the People's Republic, Xi belonged to the group known as "the princeling party" (太子党). The Shanghai clique (上海帮) was led by former general secretary Jiang Zemin and his supporters based in the city. The Youth League faction (团派), consisting of those with a background in the party's powerful Youth League, included Hu Jintao. Xi had succeeded in getting the support of all these important political networks. In addition to his indisputable merits, he had demonstrated his ability to build bridges and find compromises. These skills contributed to his rise upward in the party hierarchy.

## Behind Every Great Man . . .

Xi got married again in 1987, this time to the popular folk singer Peng Liyuan. Undoubtedly the marriage benefitted his career, even if allegedly it was a long-distance relationship during the twenty years he worked in Fujian and she had her career in Beijing. For the first twenty years of their marriage, until Xi became vice president in 2008, he was known as "Peng Liyuan's husband." A beautiful and charismatic major general in the PLA's music corps, she was famed for her powerful and riveting propaganda songs. She was far more used to being a public figure than Xi and gave her husband advice on how to behave in public in order to be liked.[52]

But it was far from love at first sight for Peng. When she met Xi for the first time, she was not impressed: she thought his style and appearance were not smart and his clothes out-of-date. However, this poor first impression was soon more than overcome by the way he spoke to her. The first question most people asked when they met her was how much she earned per performance. Peng shares this experience with most Chinese: asking how much you earn is common in China. Xi, in contrast, asked her about music in general and the skills she needed for her work specifically. Apparently he did not know who she was, not watching television much, he said, and was more interested in her as a person than as a celebrity. After a few months they got married. The relationship developed so quickly and discreetly that one of the guests in the modest reception after the wedding exclaimed, "What is *she* doing here?" upon seeing the famous Peng.[53]

In several instances Peng played an important part in Xi's career climbing, among other things by knitting decisive bonds to the Shanghai clique.[54] Zeng Qinghuai, brother of then Vice President Zeng Qinghong, is one example. A top bureaucrat in the Ministry of Culture and genuinely interested in the performing arts, he had taken Peng under his wing. Peng realized the importance of building useful relationships and arranged for Xi to meet one of the Shanghai clique's key players, Zeng Qinghong.

Another example is Jiang Zemin himself. After he was pushed out of his position as leader of the Central Military Commission in

2004, he decided to lick his wounds during a longer stay in picturesque Hangzhou, the capital of Zhejiang Province. Xi, who was party secretary there, got no word of this as Jiang was without title and the stay was to be an unofficial one. Nonetheless, Jiang's people told Peng, thereby giving Xi the chance to knit bonds to and impress Jiang, a chance he exploited to the maximum. Xi acted as Jiang's personal guide during the year he spent in Hangzhou. Knowing full well that Jiang took pride in having a good understanding of China's cultural history, Xi conversed with him about literature and art. It was supposedly during this stay that Jiang decided to support Xi on his way to the political top.[55]

Three years later, in 2007, Xi arrived at the highest level in Chinese politics, the Standing Committee of the Politburo of the Communist Party of China. With a place in China's top political leadership, he was one of only two who were young enough to be eligible to take over as general secretary and president at the next opportunity five years later. The other was Li Keqiang, party secretary in Liaoning Province and Hu Jintao's favorite to succeed him. But Xi was ranked higher than Li, a clear sign that he was meant to be the next leader.

In addition, from 2007 to 2012 Xi was awarded many important roles and tasks, another sign that he was in line—and preparation—for the post. In March 2008 he was appointed vice president and profiled outwardly as such. He made several important state visits and was given the mission of visiting the victims of the catastrophic earthquake in Sichuan Province in 2008. He was also given responsibility for several matters, among them relations with Hong Kong and Macau and preparations for the Beijing Olympics in 2008. The Olympics were a highly successful prestigious event that undoubtedly boosted Chinese self-confidence. Next Xi was picked to prepare another key event, the sixtieth anniversary of the People's Republic. Xi, with his doctorate in Marxist theory and ideological education, was chosen to lead the Central Party School, enabling him to write the report that summed up the work of the outgoing Politburo for the congress in November 2012. The report is regarded as very important within the party because it not only details what was done during that term but also points forward.

## Murder in Chongqing

Even though there was little doubt that Xi would take over the top job at the 2012 congress, he had powerful rivals in the political elite. Bo Xilai—charismatic, ambitious, stylish, charming, and among the best positioned to take over one of the top posts—was one of them. During the eighteenth party congress, he was at the center of the biggest political earthquake since the violent suppression of the 1989 demonstrations.

As party secretary in the major city of Chongqing, the world's biggest (if you include the rural areas that formally belong to it), Bo had succeeded in creating a new ideological boost not seen since Mao's time. Bo was popular both inside and outside the city, with politics and a style that distinguished him from the rest of the elite in the Communist Party. Both in and outside China there were speculations about whether Bo's model could be applied at a national level.[56] This scenario probably seemed threatening to Xi on his way to the top.

Bo's politics, called the Chongqing Model and summed up in the slogan "Sing red and strike black," marked in many areas a return to socialism under Mao. Social equalization, the building of council housing, and better working conditions were among the areas prioritized by the Bo administration. In addition to such specific measures, Chongqing experienced a series of more symbolic, ideological, and emotional measures of a socialist appearance, including, among others, prohibition of television advertising, sending high-standing civil servants to work in the countryside for the local authorities (officially they volunteered), and the mass distribution of ideological text messages. The city also literally heard a lot of red songs. Citizens were encouraged to learn and sing songs from the days of the revolution. In all 148,000 ideologically themed song competitions were arranged during Bo's first two years in office.[57]

"Strike black" referred to the campaign against the corruption and crime that was immensely widespread in Chongqing. This too was popular with the public since it targeted politicians who had got rich from crime and not just criminals. The campaign used brutal methods, and often judicial procedures were ignored in efficiency's name.[58] The sister-in-law of the leader of the city's Justice Committee was among those arrested. She ruled a network of illegal casinos, one of them located right across the street from the city's supreme court.

Bo had studied journalism and knew how to create powerful slogans and use the media to popularize his campaigns. His Chongqing Model was very popular.[59] Bo himself was very charismatic, resembling, with his jovial style and hand-tailored suits, Western politicians rather than traditional Chinese Communist Party tops. His Mao-inspired ideology had a modern packaging.

Bo and Xi had several significant things in common. Both belonged to the top of "the red aristocracy" in the People's Republic as descendants of the party elite that had taken power in 1949, a tightly knit and well-connected group. Bo senior, Bo Yibo, was even one of "the eight immortals" (八大元老), a little group that consisted of Deng Xiaoping and his seven most important advisors. Xi and Bo were thus both princes, said to have been chosen by their respective families to come under the wings of the Section for Young Cadres in the Communist Party's Organization Department, a springboard for a high-flying career in the party. Both had brilliant careers as party secretaries in large provinces to boast of and had, during the seventeenth party congress in 2007, become members of the Politburo. Both Xi and Bo were in a good position to be among the next generation's leaders.

But only Xi had also become a member of the Standing Committee of the Politburo, the highest organ of the Communist Party, which was a big defeat for Bo. This defeat was the starting point for some highly visible maneuvers, a kind of electoral campaign that Xi, and others with him, regarded as threatening. Finally, both Xi and Bo had made favorable marriages, but in Bo's case his marriage was his undoing.

In February 2012, Bo's right-hand man, Chongqing's deputy mayor and chief of police, Wang Lijun, sought refuge in the US consulate in Chengdu, panicked. The reason was the mysterious death of British businessman Neil Heywood in the now well-known three-star Lucky Holiday Hotel in Chongqing. The police had initially concluded that Heywood died of alcohol poisoning, and the corpse had been cremated before it could be autopsied. Wang Lijun, though, claimed he could prove that the Englishman had been poisoned by none other than Gu Kailai, Bo Xilai's wife. Wang shared his suspicions with Bo, who replied by slapping him, puncturing his eardrum. The police chief needed no further warning and fled immediately to the American consulate in the neighboring city. As a present to his hosts, he handed over a pile of sensitive documents that proved corruption and misgovernment under Bo's leadership and linked Bo's wife to the killing of Heywood.

After a hectic day Wang was handed over to the security authorities in Beijing. The Politburo's Standing Committee quickly convened to discuss how to handle the scandal in Chongqing. Xi is said to have been the first to break the silence after "security tsar" Zhou Yongkang, Bo's ally, started proceedings by suggesting that only Wang should be investigated. Xi's junior position meant he should not have opened the debate, but he did. He asserted that all involved in the case, implicitly also Bo and his wife, should be investigated. Prime Minister Wen Jiabao, number two on the committee, said he agreed with Xi, and subsequently Hu Jintao did too. That clinched the matter.[60] Instead of a seat on the Politburo's Standing Committee, the Communist Party's supreme organ, Bo was stripped of all his political posts and given a life sentence just before the Eighteenth National Congress opened. Gu Kailai was given a suspended death sentence for the murder of Heywood. The scandal, not least because it was unleashed by a top politician fleeing to the Americans, triggered a political earthquake that registered on the Richter scale in all corners of the globe.

But Bo Xilai was not the only one who fell out of the race in the home stretch. Ling Jihua was another one whose political careers came to a brutal end shortly before the party congress. Up to March 19, 2012, he was Hu's personal secretary and leader of the Central Committee's secretariat—as powerful a grey eminence as can be. On this day his son crashed his Ferrari Spider 458 on a motorway in Beijing. The younger Ling died instantaneously, and his two female passengers were seriously injured; one of them died later from her injuries. A car accident would not necessarily have had political consequences had the elder Ling not tried to use his position and influence to cover up the incident, probably because all three in the car were completely or partly naked.[61] When the case unraveled, many other instances of Ling's abuses of power over many years were uncovered, leading to Ling's resignation from his position in August of the same year. He was later excluded from the party, arrested, and condemned to a life sentence. Ling's position in Hu Jintao's Youth League network, an important faction within the party, was so central that the entire network was considerably weakened by the affair. Taking place half a year before the transition of power, the scandal also enfeebled Hu's chances of influencing the composition of the new party leadership.

## The Lost Decade

All the pieces fell into place for Xi in November 2012. Hu Jintao was to resign as general secretary of the Communist Party along with seven of the nine members of the Politburo's Standing Committee. China was marked by internal problems that the next generation of leaders would inherit. The final report Hu Jintao presented on his departure from the eighteenth party congress, which Xi had written, warned of "the four big dangers." These were internal problems in the Communist Party, including spiritual lassitude (精神懈怠), insufficient ability (能力不足), alienation from the people (脱离群众), and, last but not least, harmful corruption (消极腐败). Given that departing leaders customarily praised themselves and boasted of all they had achieved during their time in office, this speech was quite sensational.

Hu's words reflected a profound feeling of crisis at the top of the party. While the amazing economic growth achieved under Deng and Jiang had boosted the legitimacy of the Communist Party under the Hu-Wen administration, things had begun to progress much more slowly.[62] Decades of rapid growth had led to problems that now piled up. Hu's speech may be interpreted as an admission that the departing leaders had failed to deal with these great challenges. Hu and Wen's weak leadership was one reason for splits and factions within the party, making it hard to agree and conduct policy. Party and state were plagued by widespread corruption involving several of the top leaders and their families, even the family of Prime Minister Wen Jiabao, as it turned out later.[63] This made it harder to implement political decisions, weakened economic growth, and undermined confidence in the authorities. The scandals associated with Bo Xilai and Ling Jihua just before this critical congress shook the party to its foundations, strengthening the sense of crisis.

Outside the party too, problems were growing. The authorities faced enormous environmental issues that constituted a constant source of anxiety.[64] Not only did the degradations in themselves constitute acute problems, like lack of clean drinking water and clean air, but environmental problems were also a constant source of social unrest. Arguments that the party was a guarantor of stability and growth carried little weight when people were suffering from serious health problems, shortage of clean water, heavy air pollution, and unsafe food.

In addition, inequality was growing and becoming more visible. The Gini coefficient measures economic inequality on a scale from 0 to 1. In a society that has a 0 coefficient, all members have exactly the same income and wealth. In a society with a coefficient of 1, one person has all the income and wealth. In Hu's last term of office China's coefficient was between 0.47 and 0.49, hence above 0.4, which the United Nations considers the critical limit for social unrest.[65] The authorities also faced demographic problems. The birth-planning policy, limiting the number of children families in most parts of the population could have to one, had produced an aging society. With a lower fraction of the population of working age, it became harder to maintain economic growth. In Hu's last term, from 2007 to 2012, annual economic growth was almost halved, from 14.2 to 7.9 percent.[66]

The number of mass demonstrations was high and increasing; between 1993 and 2005 they increased tenfold, from 8,700 to 87,000 per year.[67] At this point Chinese authorities stopped publishing such statistics, probably out of fear that the high number itself would lead to even more unrest. However, a frequently quoted estimate from researchers at Tsinghua University from 2010 is 180,000 demonstrations annually.[68] Social unrest is common in several areas populated by ethnic minorities, especially Tibet and Xinjiang. Conflicts linked to autonomy in these areas were far from new under Hu, but during his tenure they reached an intensity not seen in a long time. The scenario of the Arab Spring of 2011 spreading to China kept many top politicians up at night toward the end of the Hu administration.[69] All this together made many fear the party would lose its legitimacy among the population, turning them against it.

It was now up to the next generation of leaders to tackle the issues facing China.

## Conclusion

For outsiders Beijing in the time prior to the eighteenth party congress of 2012 seems shrouded in a fog of intrigue, hassles, and horse trading. Just before the congress Xi disappeared for roughly a fortnight without any explanation. All China Hands were obsessed with finding out why he had vanished, and hypotheses flourished: Xi had back problems after he was hit with a chair during a particularly agitated party meeting; he wanted to send a signal by not meeting then–US Secretary of State Hillary Clinton, who was on a visit to Beijing; he had strained a muscle while swimming; he had been exposed to an assassination attempt—to mention a few.[70] The truth is still a well-kept secret.

After a turbulent run-up, the party congress began on November 8. A week later the seven members of the Politburo Standing Committee were presented with pomp and circumstance. Xi was general secretary and future president.

Much is unclear about how, why, and with whose support Xi finally made it all the way to the top of the Chinese Communist Party, which by then had grown from its original 53 members at its founding a century earlier to 85 million members. Kerry Brown, professor at King's College London, has described the process as a complex, invisible, chemical reaction that "belonged more to the realm of magic than political science."[71] However, the process is far from magic but rather takes place inside a closed system that outsiders have little insight into. Formally it is the National party congress that elects the Central Committee, the Politburo, the Politburo's Standing Committee, and the general secretary. However, in practice this is purely a formality. Prior to the formal processes, the new leaders have been picked in backroom deals among sitting members of the Politburo and previous party tops.

There are several theories as to why Xi was selected. One is that Xi Jinping was picked by Jiang Zemin in the same way that Hu Jintao was picked by Deng Xiaoping. Sitting leaders chose not their successors but their successor's successor. In Chinese this is called "every second generation appointment" (隔代指定)—in other words, "grandfather picks grandchild."[72] The purpose of such a system, to the extent it exists, is to secure the balance of power between factions within the party and thereby arrange matters for an orderly change of leader. If this is correct, then Hu Jintao preferred Li Keqiang, but Jiang Zemin won with his candidate, Xi Jinping. A competing theory is that Deng Xiaoping had picked both Jiang and Hu and that Xi's appointment marked the first time the sitting party elite had a real choice and could appoint the best-suited leader.[73]

Undoubtedly Xi had his strengths. First, he had solid merits to show. Today's political system is built on the Chinese tradition of meritocracy, which is deeply rooted in Confucianism and the imperial tradition of entrance by exam. Nowadays the powerful Organization Department keeps an eye on minor cadres all over the country to evaluate their achievements from an early age.[74] The aim is to identify future leaders. Xi was among those who distinguished themselves by their efforts and results while climbing the political hierarchy. He had led provinces the size of some of Europe's biggest countries, gaining solid experience in administration and economic reform. He had also had some experience and connection with the military.

A video that spread like wildfire across China in 2013 pictures Xi's meritocratic rise to power. It claims that before he became general secretary, Xi had held seventeen different political posts and governed a total of 150 million people over forty years. Through these years "Xi navigated through all kinds of currents and shoals" before he was found worthy of the country's top post.[75] Such a road to the top, where Xi had gathered experience and shown what he was good for, contrasts with that of many Western politicians whose road to power is merely a popularity contest.

Second, Xi was someone all the party tops and networks could agree on. He was not too directly connected to any faction. Throughout his career he had avoided offending influential groups or individuals in the party and instead distinguished himself as a consensus builder. Xi had steered clear of political scandals and, in contrast with many other party members, shown his firmness of principle, strength, and integrity in steering clear of corruption. This invited confidence.[76] Xi had demonstrated his ability to build compromise, and he became a candidate everyone at the top of the party could accept.[77]

Third, Xi had "blue blood" in his veins as the son of a revolutionary hero and member of the first generation of leaders of the People's Republic. The theory of "political DNA," popular in the Mao period, had got a new spring in China.[78] Descendants of the red aristocracy like to claim, "If the father is a hero, the son is a hero. If the father is a counterrevolutionary, the son is a rotten egg" (老子英雄儿好汉, 老子反动儿混蛋). Or as we would say, "Like father, like son." As the son of a hero, Xi could be relied on to have the right ideology. Had he not studied it in depth for his doctorate? Was his loyalty not proven? Xi certainly seemed to have a genuine belief in the party's historic role and mission. In the words of French political sociologist Pierre Bourdieu, Xi's family background gave him "symbolic and social capital."[79] His connection with the origins of the People's Republic gave him considerable symbolic capital (prestige, reputation, fame) as this is something that gave him recognition and legitimacy within the Chinese population.[80] At the same time, on account of his upbringing and background, he had accumulated social capital, especially in the form of a network and connections with the party elite.

Last, the top echelon of the party saw personal qualities in Xi that had been missed in Hu Jintao. Hu was stiff, without character, and awkward, while Xi was calm, relaxed, and self-confident. Now one talked of "the lost decade" under Hu, and the party elite agreed that a far stronger leader was needed, one who could tackle the heap of challenges that were mounting up for China, one who could create renewed enthusiasm and support for the party among the population.

## Notes

1. Among researchers with the lowest estimates is Peng Xizhe, who thinks 23 million Chinese died: "Demographic Consequences of the Great Leap Forward in China's Provinces," *Population and Development Review*

13, no. 4 (1987): 649. Frank Dikötter has the highest estimate of at least 45 million, see *Mao's Great Famine: The History of China's Most Devastating Catastrophe, 1958–62* (New York: Walker & Company, 2010), 333.

2. Roderick MacFarquhar and Michael Schoenhals, *Mao's Last Revolution* (Cambridge, MA: Belknap Press of Harvard University Press, 2008), 8–13.

3. CIA, *Intelligence Report: The Cultural Revolution and the Ninth Party Congress*, CIA, October 1, 1969, www.cia.gov/library/readingroom/docs /CIA-RDP85T00875R001000010037-6.pdf.

4. MacFarquhar and Schoenhals, *Mao's Last Revolution*, 2.

5. MacFarquhar and Schoenhals, *Mao's Last Revolution*, 103.

6. Helena K. Rene, *China's Sent-Down Generation: Public Administration and the Legacies of Mao's Rustication Program* (Washington, DC: Georgetown University Press, 2013), 72.

7. See, for example, "Source List and Detailed Death Tolls for the Primary Megadeaths of the Twentieth Century," Necrometrics, http://necrometrics .com/20c5m.htm#Mao; "How Many Died? New Evidence Suggests Far Higher Numbers for the Victims of Mao Zedong's Era," *Washington Post*, June 17, 1994, www.washingtonpost.com/archive/politics/1994/07/17/how -many-died-new-evidence-suggests-far-higher-numbers-for-the-victims -of-mao-zedongs-era/01044df5-03dd-49f4-a453-a033c5287bce.

8. Agnès Andrésy, *Xi Jinping: Red China, the Next Generation* (Lanham, MD: University Press of America, 2016), 12–13; Cheng Li, *Chinese Politics in the Xi Jinping Era: Reassessing Collective Leadership* (Washington, DC: Brookings Institution Press, 2016), 320.

9. Joseph Torigian in Smith and Lim, "Xi Dada and Daddy."

10. Nathan, "Who Is Xi?"

11. See, for example, François Bougon, *Inside the Mind of Xi Jinping* (London: C. Hurst & Co. Ltd., 2018), 50–51.

12. Conversation with Professor Jean-Philippe Beja, Sciences Po, Paris, June 11, 2019; "Xi Jinping: My Road to Politics: Interview from Summer 2000," *Zhonghua Ernü*, translated by Nordic Institute for Asian Studies, August 2000, https://www.asiaportal.info/xi-jinping-my-road-into-politics/.

13. Xi Jinping's foreword to Anonymous, *Liangjiahe Village: A Story of Chinese President Xi Jinping* (Xian: Shaanxi People's Publishing House Co. Ltd, 2018). Shaanxi Province is part of the Loess Plateau, in the highlands in the transition between the northern Chinese plain and the mountains in Mongolia to the north and Tibet to the east.

14. See, for example, Bougon, *Inside the Mind of Xi Jinping*, 45–70.

15. The visit in 2015 is described in detail in Anonymous, *Liangjiahe Village*.

16. "Speech by H. E. Xi Jinping President of the People's Republic of China at the Welcoming Dinner Hosted by Local Governments and Friendly Organizations in the United States, Seattle, 22 September, 2015,"

Ministry of Foreign Affairs, the People's Republic of China, www.fmprc.gov
.cn/mfa_eng/topics_665678/2015zt/xjpdmgjxgsfwbcxlhgcl70znxlfh/201510
/t20151013_705321.html.

17. Quoted in "A Tree a Thousand Feet Tall Knows Its Roots: Unforget-
table Liangjiahe," *China Story*, 2018, www.chinastory.cn/PCywdbk/english
/v1/detail/20190729/1012700000042741564129534711300378_1.html.

18. Ji Xianlin, *The Cowshed: Memories of the Cultural Revolution* (New
York: New York Review Books, 1998).

19. Margaret Chu, "A Catholic Voice out of Communist China," Cardinal
Kung Foundation, http://www.cardinalkungfoundation.org/ar/pdf/ACatholic
VoiceOutofChina.pdf .

20. In *Inside the Mind of Xi Jinping*, 56, François Bougon argues that Xi's
successful career is due to the self-confidence and ability to meet challenges
that he acquired in this period.

21. Quoted in Edward Wong, "Tracing the Myth of a Chinese Leader to
Its Roots," *New York Times*, February 16, 2011, www.nytimes.com/2011
/02/17/world/asia/17village.html.

22. Conversation with Professor Jean-Philippe Beja at Sciences Po, Paris,
June 11, 2019; Andrésy, *Xi Jinping*, 24; Bougon, *Inside the Mind of Xi Jinping*, 59–60.

23. François Bougon argues that Xi has tried to clear his family's honour
in *Inside the Mind of Xi Jinping*, 52.

24. See, for example, Andrésy, *Xi Jinping*, 25.

25. Willy Wo-Lap Lam, in *Chinese Politics in the Era of Xi Jinping:
Renaissance, Reform, or Retrogression?* (New York: Routledge, 2015), 35,
describes Xi as the best of his generation to hold together different factions
and power blocks.

26. Anonymous, *Liangjiahe Village*, 108.

27. Li, *Chinese Politics in the Xi Jinping Era*, 308.

28. Kerry Brown, *The World According to Xi: Everything You Need to Know
About the New China* (London: I. B. Taurus, 2018), 12–13; Richard McGregor,
"Party Man. Xi Jinping's Quest to Dominate China," *Foreign Policy*, August
14, 2019, www.foreignaffairs.com/articles/china/2019-08-14/party-man.

29. Lam, *Chinese Politics*, 43.

30. Cheng Li, "Xi Jinping's Inner Circle," *China Leadership Monitor*,
July 28, 2014, www.hoover.org/sites/default/files/research/docs/clm44cl.pdf;
François Godement, "Portrait of Xi Jinping—President of the People's
Republic of China," Institut Montaigne, November 22, 2018, www.institut
montaigne.org/en/blog/portrait-xi-jinping-president-peoples-republic-china.

31. Desmond Shum, *Red Roulette: An Insider's Story of Wealth, Power,
Corruption and Vengeance in Today's China* (New York: Scribner, 2021),
239–240.

32. Lam, *Chinese Politics*, 43.

33. Kerry Brown, *CEO, China: The Rise of Xi Jinping* (London: I. B. Tauris, 2016), 64–65.

34. Andrésy, *Xi Jinping*, 33.

35. Naughton, "Deng Xiaoping."

36. Clyde D. Stoltenberg, "China's Special Economic Zones: Their Development and Prospects," *Asian Survey* 24, no. 6 (1984).

37. "Xi Jinping's Political Career and Rise in the Communist Party," *Facts and Details*, http://factsanddetails.com/china/cat2/4sub5/item2855.html.

38. Minnie Chan, "Xi Jinping Sharpened his Political Skills in Fujian," *South China Morning Post*, October 2, 2012, www.scmp.com/news/china/article/1068111/xi-jinping-sharpened-his-political-skills-fujian.

39. Brown, *CEO, China*, 69.

40. Brown, *CEO, China*, 72; Bo Zhiyue, "Chinas Fifth-Generation Leaders: Characteristics of the New Elite and Pathways to Leadership," in Robert S. Ross and Jo Inge Bekkevold (eds.), *China in the Era of Xi Jinping: Domestic and Foreign Policy Challenges* (Washington, DC: Georgetown University Press, 2016).

41. "Xi Jinping's 17 Years in Fujian," China.org.cn, October 21, 2012, www.china.org.cn/china/2012-11/21/content_27179199.htm.

42. McGregor, "Party Man."

43. François Bougon argues for this in *Inside the Mind of Xi Jinping*, 62.

44. Lam, *Chinese Politics*, 38.

45. See, for example, Minxin Pei, quoted in Tom Hancock and Liu Nicolle, "Top Chinese Officials Plagiarised Doctoral Dissertations," *Financial Times*, February 27, 2019; Stephen Thompson, "Plagiarism and Xi Jinping," *Asia Sentinel*, September 25, 2013, www.asiasentinel.com/p/plagiarism-and-xi-jinping.

46. Lam, *Chinese Politics*, 52–55.

47. CEIC Data: www.ceicdata.com/en.

48. Brown, *CEO, China*, 74.

49. Christina Zhou and Sean Mantesso, "Chinese President Xi Jinping's Astonishing Rise to Become One of the World's Most Powerful People," *ABC News*, March 6, 2019, www.abc.net.au/news/2019-03-06/the-astonishing-rise-of-chinese-president-xi-jinping/10794486.

50. Ding Zinghao, former president of Shanghai Institute of American Studies, quoted in Lam, *Chinese Politics*, 34–35.

51. See, for example, Cheng Li, "The Powerful Factions Among China's Rulers," Brookings Institution, November 5, 2012, www.brookings.edu/articles/the-powerful-factions-among-chinas-rulers; Alice Miller, "The Trouble with Factions," *China Leadership Monitor*, March 16, 2015, https://www.hoover.org/sites/default/files/research/docs/clm46am-2.pdf.

52. Lam, *Chinese Politics*, 40.

53. Andrésy, *Xi Jinping*, 45.

54. Lam, *Chinese Politics*, 57.

55. Lam, *Chinese Politics*, 58; Andrésy, *Xi Jinping*, 58.

56. Brown, *CEO, China*, 92; Bruce J. Dickson, *The Dictator's Dilemma: The Chinese Communist Party's Strategy for Survival* (New York: Oxford University Press, 2016), 85–86; Jude D. Blanchette, *China's New Red Guards. The Return of Radicalism and the Rebirth of Mao Zedong* (New York: Oxford University Press, 2019), 110.

57. "两千机关干部颂歌献给党" [Two thousand officials sing odes to the party], *Sina*, http://news.sina.com.cn/o/2008-07-01/031014096113s.shtml; Zhun Xu, "The Chongqing Event and Its Implications," *Economic and Political Weekly* 47, no. 16 (2012), www.epw.in/journal/2012/16/commentary/chongqing-event-and-its-implications.html; Blanchette, *China's New Red Guards*, 112–113.

58. For more on Bo's rule, see, for example, John Ganault, *The Rise and Fall of the House of Bo* (Melbourne: Penguin Random House, Australia, 2012).

59. See, for example, "一个重庆人谈谈重庆唱红打黑及民生工程背后的真实!" [A Chongqinger tells the truth behind Chongqing's "sing red, strike black" and the Project for People's Livelihood], *Tianya*, March 7, 2012, http://bbs.tianya.cn/post-free-2416030-1.shtml.

60. Shum, *Red Roulette*, 242–243.

61. Dickson, *The Dictator's Dilemma*, 88; "How Son's Death in a High-Speed Car Crash Led to Powerful Chinese Official's Fall from Grace," *South China Morning Post*, December 23, 2014, www.scmp.com/news/china/article/1668151/how-sons-death-high-speed-car-crash-led-powerful-chinese-officials-fall.

62. See, for example, Cheng Li and Eve Cary, "The Last Year of Hu's Leadership: Hu's to Blame?" Jamestown Foundation, December 20, 2011, https://jamestown.org/program/the-last-year-of-hus-leadership-hus-to-blame. For a more nuanced version of the negative picture presented here, see Jude Howell and Jane Duckett, "Reassessing the Hu-Wen Era: A Golden Age or Lost Decade for Social Policy in China?" *China Quarterly* 237 (2018): 1–14, www.cambridge.org/core/journals/china-quarterly/article/reassessing-the-huwen-era-a-golden-age-or-lost-decade-for-social-policy-in-china/8270E2AF1D13DE32715A5598414D064F.

63. For an eyewitness account of corruption practice at this time, see Shum, *Red Roulette*.

64 See, for example, Deng Yanhua and Yang Guobin, "Pollution and Protest in China: Environmental Mobilization in Context," *China Quarterly* 214 (2013), www.jstor.org/stable/23509600?seq=1.

65. "China Gini Coefficient," CEIC Data, www.ceicdata.com/en/china/resident-income-distribution/gini-coefficient; Mamta Badkar, "Here's How We Know Beijing Is Terrified About Social Unrest," *Business Insider*,

November 8, 2012, www.businessinsider.com/heres-how-we-know-beijing-is-terrified-about-social-rest-2012-11.

66. "People's Republic of China," International Monetary Fund, www.imf.org/en/Countries/CHN.

67. For more about protest actions in this period, see Tong Yanqi and Lei Shaohua (eds.), *Social Protest in Contemporary China, 2003–2010: Transitional Pains and Regime Legitimacy* (New York: Routledge, 2014).

68. Lynette H. Ong and Christian Goebel, "Social Unrest in China," in Kerry Brown (ed.), *China and the EU in Context* (London: Palgrave MacMillan, 2014), 178–213.

69. Stig Stenslie and Marte Kjær Galtung, "The Arab Spring Seen from Beijing," *Internasjonal Politikk* 4 (2014): 452–466.

70. Ian Johnson, "Communist Leader's Absence Sets Off Rumor Mills in China," *New York Times*, September 10, 2012, www.nytimes.com/2012/09/11/world/asia/xi-jinping-chinas-presumptive-new-leader-mysteriously-absent.html; Brown, *The World According to Xi*, 22.

71. Brown, *CEO, China*, 92.

72. See, for example, Zheng Wang, "The Next Hu," Wilson Center, December 20, 2012, www.wilsoncenter.org/article/the-next-hu.

73. See, for example, Jean-Pierre Cabestan, "Is Xi Jinping the Reformist Leader China Needs?" *China Perspectives*, October 2012, https://journals.openedition.org/chinaperspectives/5969.

74. Andrésy, *Xi Jinping*, 33 and 144.

75. Bougon, *Inside the Mind of Xi Jinping*, 47.

76. Andrésy, *Xi Jinping*, 59.

77. Conversations with Professor Jean-Pierre Cabestan, Hong Kong Baptist University, Hong Kong, November 2018; with Professor Jean-Philippe Beja, Science Po, Paris, June 2019. Steve Tsang supports this theory; see "Chinese President Xi Jinping's Astonishing Rise to Become One of the World's Most Powerful People," *ABC News*, March 6, 2019, www.abc.net.au/news/2019-03-06/the-astonishing-rise-of-chinese-president-xi-jinping/10794486.

78. Nathan, "Who Is Xi?"

79. See, for example, Pierre Bourdieu, "The Forms of Capital," in John G. Richardson (ed.), *Handbook of Theory and Research for the Sociology of Education* (New York: Greenwood Press, 1986); Pierre Bourdieu, *Language and Symbolic Power* (Cambridge, MA: Harvard University Press, 1991).

80. For the role "The Yellow Earth" has in Chinese collective memory, see Bougon, *Inside the Mind of Xi Jinping*, 53.

# 3

## Concentrating Power

IN OCTOBER 2017, ONLY FIVE YEARS AFTER BECOMING GENERAL secretary of the Chinese Communist Party (CCP), Xi Jinping began to resemble the old emperors who were seen as the rulers of "all under the heaven." At the nineteenth party congress in Beijing, *Xi's Thoughts About Socialism with a Chinese Character for a New Era* (习近平新时代中国特色社会主义思想), shortened to *Xi Jinping's Thoughts* (习近平思想), were included in the CCP's constitution. Xi thus became the first leader since Mao Zedong to have his ideology inscribed in the constitution while he was still in power. Xi was also mentioned by name in the constitution, something his predecessors Jiang Zemin and Hu Jintao never were. This honor is reserved for the gold stars among the Chinese leaders—Mao, Deng Xiaoping, and Xi.

Xi's dominant position was emphatically confirmed by a critical change in the law five months later. In March 2018 a majority of the delegates to the National People's Congress, China's parliament and legislative assembly, voted on a proposal to delete a sentence in the constitution restricting a president to two terms: out of a total of 2,964 delegates, 2 voted against the change, and 3 abstained.[1] Deng, who had ensured this restriction became law to avoid a new Mao, probably turned in his grave. By insisting on this limit, Deng had paved the way for an orderly change of leadership, the weak point of any authoritarian regime. The deletion made it possible for Xi to continue as president after 2023—and perhaps to be China's leader for life. How did Xi become so powerful?

## Chairman of Everything

Xi Jinping was immediately served all the top posts on a silver platter. At the 2012 party congress, he took over as general secretary of the Chinese Communist Party and chairman of the Central Military Commission. Hu Jintao, Xi's immediate predecessor, had in his time a far weaker start. At the sixteenth party congress in 2002, Hu took over the post of general secretary of the Chinese Communist Party and became president the following year. But the departing leader, Jiang Zemin, was the party's star. Not only did he fill the Politburo and the Politburo's Standing Committee with his allies from Shanghai, but Jiang stayed on as chairman of the Central Military Commission. Thus, his power remained even after he left the offices of general secretary and president, allowing him to largely restrict Hu's chances of carrying through his policies.[2]

Xi, however, was given a far more favorable starting point. So further steps were rapidly taken to centralize and strengthen his power. In November 2013, just one year after his ascent to power, two new superstructures were erected that lorded it over existing institutions. One was for reform, the other for national security, both chaired by Xi.

Through the newly established Central Comprehensively Deepening Reforms Commission, Xi could give direct political guidelines for important work on economic, cultural, and social reform and supervise the execution of the reform plans. The commission could shove political initiatives past other party leaders, thereby helping Xi consolidate his control over China's enormous government apparatus. This broke with previous practice in which economy and reform had been the prime minister's domain. Under Hu Jintao, Prime Minister Wen Jiabao ruled the economy, giving him major influence. When Xi came to power, he himself took over the chair of the leaders' group for the economy, which many China observers interpreted as a marginalization of the then number two in the party hierarchy,

Prime Minister Li Keqiang. The same observers meant that the establishment of the Xi-led commission further undermined Li.

In the same way Xi took direct control over no less than the police, the People's Liberation Army, the security services, and the justice system through the newly established National Security Commission. Under Hu these had almost constituted an autonomous empire under Zhou Yongkang, who at the time led the party's Central Political and Judicial Commission and was thereby one of China's most powerful men. Zhou and several of his allies were caught for abuse of power and corruption at roughly the same time as Xi came to power. This made it possible for Xi to take control over China's huge repressive apparatus. He ensured that the National Security Commission obeyed only his orders and would not operate on behalf of any party organ, not even the Politburo's Standing Committee.

At the time of writing, Xi has more than a dozen formal leadership positions (see Table 3.1), a number that has increased steadily since he came to power. He is general secretary of China's Communist Party, China's president, chairman of the Central Military Commission, and chairman of the National Security Commission, as well as heading a series of other central commissions, among others, for economic reform, foreign policy, and military reform. All these positions give him direct control over the party, the state, and the armed forces. In other words, Xi is the entire British or US government in one and the same person, and even more so. It is therefore not strange that he has been nicknamed "Chairman of Everything."[3]

## The Power of Language

In addition to holding all these positions Xi can decorate himself with a whole series of official and semiofficial titles. These are used in official party documents—for example, the party constitution and communiqués from party congresses and plenum meetings. The Central Committee's plenum meeting is the Communist Party's supreme organ between party congresses and is held at least once a year. Party congresses are held every fifth year. In the United Kingdom and the United States, such titles are unknown, but in the Chinese party

**Table 3.1 Xi's Positions in the Party, State, and Armed Forces**

General Secretary of China's Communist Party
President of China
Chairman of the Central Military Commission
Chairman of the National Security Commission
Chairman of the Central Commission for Comprehensively Deepening
  Reforms
Chairman of the Central Commission for the Economy and Finance
Chairman of the National Audit Office
Chairman of the Central Cyberspace Affairs Commission
Chairman of the Central Committee for Foreign Policy
Chairman of the Central Committee for Comprehensive Law-Based
Governance
Chairman of the Central Leadership Group for Military Reform
Chairman of the Central Leadership Group for Loyalty to
  Our Foundation Mission Campaign
Supreme Commander of the Central Military Committee's Combined
  Operations Office

*Source:* The titles are from Nis Grünberg, "The CCP's Nerve Center: Xi Jinping and His Aides Hold Sway over Powerful Core Institutions," Mercator Institute for China Studies, October 30, 2019, https://merics.org/en/graphic/ccps-nerve-center; Sebastian Heilmann and Matthias Stepan (eds.), "China's Core Executive Leadership Styles, Structures and Processes Under Xi Jinping," MERICS Papers on China 1 (2016), 77, https://www.stiftung-mercator.de/media/user_upload/MPOC_Chinas CoreExecutive.pdf.

state these are important markers of power and the object of long, internal struggles. Following the development of how Xi is mentioned and what titles he is given provides a window into Chinese elite politics and a measure of the top leader's personal power.

In connection with the congress in October 2017, Xi was written into the party constitution as "the core of the leadership" (领导核心). This title emphasizes that he is the undisputed leader, whom all party members and Chinese are subordinate to. He thus became the fourth "core" after Mao, Deng, and Jiang. In addition, the constitution stated that the party's 96 million members must all uphold Xi Jinping's core position. In other words, according to the law, one must be loyal to Xi.

The constitution of China's Communist Party states, "Remember the need to maintain political integrity, think the big picture, maintain the leadership core, keep the line, hold firm the Central Committee's authority and centralised unified leadership with Comrade Xi Jinping at the core."[4]

In the communiqué to the Central Committee's fifth plenum, held in October 2020, the party rhetoric exalts Xi even higher. For the first time he is referred to as the "core navigator and ship's captain" (核心领航掌舵). The party rhetoric frequently uses marine metaphors for the challenges the party state faces. Mao was known as "the great captain" (伟大的舵手) and a ship decorated the cover of *Mao's Little Red Book*. But, after Mao, no top leader has been called "captain."[5] This new title is yet another marker of Xi's steadily more elevated position. China observers speculate whether Xi will be called "chairman" next time, as Mao was in his time, instead of the far more boring "general secretary," which has been the official title from Deng on. If this should be, Xi will be on an equal footing with the founder of the People's Republic, Mao himself.[6]

And as if that were not enough, Xi has a number of semiofficial titles. These are honorific titles that pop up in the party press. The result of political power struggles, they are often tested out in the press before perhaps gaining traction and appearing in official party documents. China observers follow such honorifics eagerly as an indication of political dynamics and power struggles at the top and of things to come. For example, in April 2017 the party press began to refer to Xi as "the people's leader" (人民领袖), a title also used for Mao. But so far the term has not been seen in official documents.[7]

## A Personality Cult

As soon as he became general secretary, a personality cult developed around Xi. Paradoxically, as mentioned in Chapter 1, Xi is not very accessible and is known for keeping his cards close to his chest. Nonetheless, he has become almost omnipresent and iconic. The Xi cult has broken with established norms in Chinese elite politics. It emphasizes his dominant position. One is tempted to interpret this as a sign that Xi has come to stay as the leader of the People's Republic of China.

The party's central propaganda apparatus got the cult going. In his first eighteen months as leader, his name appeared in the country's newspapers almost twice as often as that of any other leader since Mao.[8] And the cult soon sped up. Books, comics, pop songs, and dance steps were created to praise his rule. In 2017 the local government in Jiangxi Province asked local Christians to replace pictures of Jesus Christ with pictures of Xi Jinping.[9] Hunan TV, one of the most popular channels in the country, with youth as its target group, airs at peak time a quiz program about Xi's life and ideology.[10] In the mobile app "Study Xi to Strengthen the Country" (学习强国) users get points when they read speeches, watch videos, and take part in quizzes about Xi. Party members, state employees, and students are evaluated according to how many points they win each day and risk a reprimand if they do not fulfil the minimum required.[11]

To find an equivalent to this Xi cult, one has to cross the border into Kim Jung-un's North Korea or take a time machine back to Mao's China, precisely such a journey in time that Deng Xiaoping and the other Communist tops in their time tried to avoid. After experiencing the catastrophic consequences of Mao's despotic rule, Deng made it taboo for Chinese leaders to promote their own personalities. This came as a result of the party's critical evaluation of Mao's rule, which concluded that he got it "70 percent right, and 30 percent wrong." And the Mao cult definitely belonged to the latter percentage, the party meant. Under Xi the party has changed its mind.

## Xi's Trusted Men

Naturally leaders prefer to surround themselves with people they trust. When taking office, American presidents, CEOs, and coaches usually bring with them a completely new team to increase the chance of succeeding. Trust is the key word. Top leaders have more confidence in people they already know, whether they grew up together, went to the same school or college, or belong to the same network.[12] In this Xi is no different from top leaders anywhere. But for a leader in an authoritarian system, it is even more important than for a democratically elected leader to place his most trusted people in key positions. There is more at play, should he or she fall from power. As history has shown time after time, the worst consequence is that they, their families, and their friends will lose their lives.

China's political system is an odd symbiosis of meritocracy and network. As we mentioned in the previous chapter, meritocracy is decisive for promotion for lower cadres of the party, while personal ties are more influential the closer one gets to the top. From 2017 to 2022, five of seven members of the Politburo's Standing Committee, the party top organ, had close personal bonds to Xi. In all, fifteen of the then twenty-five members of the Politburo, the party's next most important organ, had such direct ties. Xi had appointed all present province governors and 90 percent of all province party leaders. The ties between these leaders and Xi were in many cases knitted during early formative years in Beijing and forced labor in Shaanxi during the Cultural Revolution. Others Xi met while he was climbing up the ladder in provinces such as Shaanxi, Hebei, Fujian, Zhejiang, and Shanghai or in the top central organs of the Chinese Communist Party. In comparison Xi had such close personal bonds to only five of the Politburo members from 2012 to 2017.[13]

Under the twentieth party congress arranged in October 2022, Xi Jinping further strengthened his grip on the Politburo and its Standing Committee. Half of the members of the Politburo, which was now reduced to twenty-four members, and two-thirds of the seven members of the Standing Committee were replaced. Out went all who did not have direct ties to the general secretary, most notably a handful of key figures associated with former general secretary Hu Jintao's Youth League faction, such as Li Keqiang, Wang Yang, and Hu Chunhua. The vacant seats were without exception filled by Xi loyalists. Arguably the most memorable moment from the twentieth party congress was when Hu Jintao, for reasons unknown, was escorted by two security guards out of the Great Hall of the People in disgrace, a moment that for many underscored Xi Jinping's absolute power.

Also, noteworthily, the newly appointed Politburo was the first in twenty-five years without a woman. The Chinese Communist Party has always been a most masculine institution and is even more so in Xi's China. At the grassroots, there are many active female cadres, and some reach high levels within sectors such as education, research, culture, and health. Still, there are few women high up in the party hierarchy.

In other words, Xi Jinping succeeded in placing his friends, allies, and protégés in central positions in his second period as general secretary of China's Communist Party. And they are totally dominant now in Xi's third term. As noted previously, a faction model is often used to explain Chinese politics. But because Xi loyalists are so dominant in the political elite, this is no longer so useful. The Shanghai faction and the Youth League faction associated with former leaders Jiang Zemin and Hu Jintao no longer seem so active backstage. To the extent that we can speak of factions in Xi's China, they are groups linked to Xi at the stages of his career. One group some refer to is the "Princeling Party," comprising those Xi became acquainted with in his formative years, in childhood, during the Cultural Revolution, and at university. Other groups are linked to the various provinces where Xi worked on his way up. He has especially raised many from the long period he served the party in Shaanxi Province, as well as his brief period as party secretary in Shanghai. There are now those talking about both a Shaanxi Clique and a new Shanghai faction within the Chinese Communist Party.[14] The four examples below show how Xi has surrounded himself with men (for they are all men) he got to know during the various stages of his life and political career and how these were important supporters in particular during his first decade in power.

## The Economist

Liu He is probably the one at the top of Chinese politics whom Xi has known longest. Like most of Xi's childhood friends, he too is the son of a prominent Communist leader. They grew up in the same district of the capital, played together, and went to the same schools. Liu He was born in Beijing in 1952 and is a year older than Xi. It has been claimed that the two went to the same secondary school in the 1960s, but in fact Xi attended the Bayi School and Beijing No. 25 School, while Liu attended the nearby Beijing No. 101 School in the same district. So it is likely they developed their childhood friendship in their leisure time while growing up in the same housing complex for party tops. They may have been introduced by their fathers, who probably knew each other through various posts held in Shaanxi Province.[15] Liu's career has followed two parallel tracks, academic and bureaucratic. He is among China's foremost economists, with four books and two hundred scientific papers on his curriculum vitae.[16] Since Xi came to power, he has been his most trusted economic advisor. Liu was member of the Politburo between 2017 and 2022. Since 2018, he has served as the director of the office serving the important Central Financial and Economic Affairs Commission of the Chinese Communist Party and until March 2023 as one of the deputy prime ministers of China.

## The Corruption Hunter

Wang Qishan is another of Xi's most trusted men. He illustrates perhaps more than any other the importance of personal bonds at the top of Xi's China. Their friendship dates back over half a century. They first met in a poor village in Shaanxi Province. Both were "princes" sent for forced labor in the countryside. Wang, five years Xi's elder, had arrived in the village before Xi, warmly welcomed him, and invited him to share the same cave. The two youths spent a lot of time talking about China's future. They shared the same thin bedding, and Wang loaned Xi the few books he had. Xi found a safe elder brother in Wang.[17]

In the decades that followed, Wang held a series of administrative and top political posts in, among other places, Hainan, Guangdong, and Beijing. He was appointed deputy mayor of Beijing in 2003 and mayor a year later. He became a member of the Politburo in 2007, the same year Xi was elected to the Politburo's Standing Committee. Between 2012 and 2017 Wang was a member of the Politburo's Standing Committee and secretary of the Central Commission for Disciplinary Inspection. Thus, he was in charge of Xi's anticorruption campaign. He was also central in designing and handling China's foreign policy. From 2018 to 2023 he served as vice president of China. China observers have often considered Wang "the second most powerful man in China," second only to Xi Jinping. Despite no longer being a member of the Standing Committee, Xi's right-hand man still has considerable influence.

## The Personnel Manager

Chen Xi is the third member of the political elite close to Xi. They got to know each other as study and flat mates at Tsinghua University from 1975 to 1979. Both were so-called worker-peasant-soldier-students and studied chemical technology. They immediately became good friends, sharing an interest in sports and liking to talk about politics. Xi is said to have enlisted Chen into the Communist Party in 1978. After sitting his exams, Chen continued as a researcher at Tsinghua for thirty years, while Xi disappeared into the provinces, where he held various leadership positions for the party. Despite their quite different career paths, they remained in close touch, meeting often in Beijing and other places. Xi and his wife were also fixed inventory at the annual reunions of the Tsinghua year group.[18] As soon as Xi became a member of the Politburo's Standing Committee, he saw to it that his old friend was appointed deputy minister of education. The year after Xi became general secretary of China's Communist Party, Chen's road to the top continued. Between 2017 and 2022, Chen served as a member of the Politburo and a secretary of the secretariat of the Chinese Communist Party. Since 2017, Chen has been head of the important Organization Department for the party, thus Xi's human resources manager and president of the Central Party School.

## The Thinker

Wang Huning is the fourth person who is very close to Xi. Wang distinguishes himself from the other three members of the inner circle in that he was well established in the political elite before Xi and is therefore not someone China's leader has taken to the top. Since Xi was brought to Beijing in 2007, the two of them have worked closely together. Wang is described as a classic Chinese bookworm with good ideas.[19] He studied French and international politics in the 1970s before becoming history's youngest dean at Fudan University in Shanghai. In 1995 Wang started his career as party theoretician, in Chinese called a "pen shaft" (笔杆子). He was fetched into and climbed the ranks of the Chinese Communist Party's Office for Official Publications and Reports, becoming its director in 2002.

Wang is said to be the brain behind the central ideological concepts attributed to three leaders: "the three representations" (Jiang Zemin), "scientific development" (Hu Jintao), and "the Chinese dream" (Xi Jinping). We shall have a closer look at the last of these in Chapter 5.[20] That Wang has managed to be a central advisor for three successive Chinese leaders is a unique achievement; it probably reflects that he is flexible and not regarded as a threat by anyone. Because of his career, he has acquired the nicknames "chief advisor in Zhongnanhai" and "China's Henry Kissinger."[21] After Xi came to power in 2012, Wang was often seen accompanying him, and he was quickly identified as a member of the new leader's inner circle. In 2017 he was appointed as one of the seven members of the Politburo's Standing Committee, underlining his closeness to Xi.

Both are concerned with the party and its ideology, and both are sober men who are more concerned about the party's health than their own enrichment. The latter may be why they were attracted to each other. All the corruption scandals prior to Xi's takeover had threatened to undermine confidence in the party. Wang may well have sought Xi because they shared a concern about this. Wang Huning is known for his down-to-earth style, being in that way rather like former Norwegian prime minister Einar Gerhardsen, who despite his position lived in a perfectly ordinary flat and had a very modest style of living. In Beijing there are many stories about Wang's sobriety. For instance, in the 1980s he was offered a bigger and better flat suitable for one who had risen within the university system. Wang refused politely, saying there were surely others who had greater use for it. In all likelihood, Wang wanted to spend his time reading rather than moving boxloads of books.[22]

## The Head of Security

It is worth noting Lieutenant General Wang Shaojun in addition to these. While the others are stars on the political stage, Wang operates in the wings as head of the Communist Party's Central Security Bureau, a post he has held since 2015. The bureau is responsible for the security of China's top civil and military leadership and their families. As well as handling their personal security, the bureau is responsible for protecting the offices and living quarters of the leaders in Zhong-nanhai. The bureau also guards key sites such as the Mao Mau-soleum, the People's Congress Hall, and the Tiananmen Square. The bureau, which can be compared with the US president's secret serv-ice, is vital for any party chairman, not least for Xi Jinping. The unit protects Xi against coup and assassination, and through it he controls the physical environment of the other party leaders. The head of the bureau must then enjoy Xi's complete trust. While Mao had his loyal security boss Wang Dongxing, Xi has his trusted Wang Shaojun.

Before becoming head of the bureau in 2015, Wang was one of the next in command and a personal bodyguard for Xi.[23] In other words, Xi and Wang had worked closely together daily for many years. In the wake of security tsar Zhou Yongkang's dramatic fall, more or less plausible rumors about at least six attempts on Xi's life made the rounds.[24] Xi, who is highly concerned about his personal security because of all the enemies he has made with his anticorrup-tion campaign, made sure once he became party leader that his loyal personal guard was promoted to security boss.

Through his trusted men, Xi has firm control of, among other things, the party apparatus, the propaganda machine, the courts, the armed forces, the economy and administration, homeland security, and international relations. Xi's inner circle is small and tight. It consists of persons the leader knows he can rely on as they have proved their personal loyalty to him. It is these Xi spends most of his time with, and apart from them, there are few who have access to the leader.

## Hunting Flies and Tigers

In his inaugural speech as general secretary of the Chinese Commu-nist Party on November 15, 2012, Xi warned that corruption under-mines Chinese faith in the party and the country's economic devel-opment.[25] Directly afterward Xi got Wang Qishan to swing the party whip. As head of the Central Commission for Disciplinary Inspec-tion, which is in charge of investigating all breaches of party rules, including corruption, he launched the biggest anticorruption campaign since the Cultural Revolution. It was a necessary measure to put the brakes on galloping corruption and abuse of power and to strengthen the party's legitimacy.[26] At the same time Xi has used it to remove bothersome political rivals.[27]

The scope of the campaign is massive. In October 2017 the Disciplinary Commission published statistics for the campaign's first year. Almost 2.7 million civil servants had been investigated, 1.5 million had been punished, and 58,000 were still being processed by the courts. Among those investigated were 440 top officials, that is, high-ranking leaders in the party state and armed forces.[28] As the figures show, both those Xi refers to as tigers (top officeholders) and those he calls "flies" (low-ranking officials) were targets of the campaign. On December 6, less than a month after Xi Jinping's inauguration speech, Li Chuncheng, deputy party secretary in Sichuan Province and mayor of Chengdu, became the first tiger to be hunted down. Li was found guilty of abusing power and enriching himself and his allies in the ten years he had governed the city. During that time Liu had bulldozed half this historic city and erected modern skyscrapers. He was known as "Li the destroyer of the city," a powerful man who controlled a number of local media, as well as commercial and property-development firms. He was condemned to thirteen years in prison for his misdeeds.

Li's fall was a sign of what was to come—namely, the case against Zhou Yongkang. In his time Li had risen up the party ladder while Zhou was party secretary in Sichuan. Zhou was now one of China's most powerful men. He was a member of the Politburo's Standing Committee and was in charge of the judicial system and security apparatus. By virtue of his position, he had built his own private empire. Known as China's security tsar, he controlled a comprehensive network and precious, sensitive information about important people. Zhou had made himself unpopular within the elite by using the security apparatus against his political opponents, among other things, by communications surveillance of other party leaders.[29] In accordance with regulations at the time, Zhou had to retire in 2012, but he might still have exerted influence through the man expected to replace him, Bo Xilai. But after Bo's dramatic fall, described in Chapter 2, Zhou rapidly lost power.

It became clear that the Central Commission for Disciplinary Inspection had Zhou in its sights as more and more of his allies came under investigation. In July 2014, it became known that Zhou himself was under investigation. The authorities claimed they had seized values that he had illegally appropriated worth £10.5 billion or $12.4 billion, a sum greater than Albania's gross national product.³⁰ Arrested and excluded from the party, Zhou was exposed to a public smear campaign in the state media, charging him with sexual immorality and even having orchestrated the theft of organs from inmates in the prisons he was in charge of. Other party tops condemned him.

In 2015 he was sentenced to life imprisonment. Since then, he has been in Qincheng, a prison an hour's drive north of Beijing. He serves time here with other former party leaders, such as Bo Xilai's wife, Gu Kailai, condemned for poisoning Neil Heywood. So does Bo's henchman, former police chief Wang Lijun. China's tiger cage is where ex-leaders are jailed. During the history of the People's Republic, those who have lost the struggle for power, corrupt politicians, newspaper editors who have criticized the central authorities, leaders of the democracy movement at Tiananmen Square in 1989, and Mao's power-hungry widow have served time here. In Qincheng, China's most notorious prisoners still enjoy a privileged existence with better food, beds, and cells than other prisoners. Rumor has it that Zhou Yongkang has time to grow fruit and vegetables in a garden near his cell, while Bo Xilai wears a suit instead of the obligatory prison uniform.³¹

By starting a corruption investigation against Zhou and several other retired party tops, Xi Jinping broke an unwritten rule that retired members of the Politburo's Standing Committee were immune to prosecution.³² Not since the fall of the notorious Gang of Four after Mao's death had such a high-ranking member of the party been prosecuted and condemned. By doing so Xi removed a vital condition for the circulation of leaders at the top of the party. When retired members of the Standing Committee are no longer secured against prosecution, it is far from certain that they will dare retire from their posts.

The utmost consequence could be that Xi too might be prosecuted once he is no longer in power.

Other party tops have fallen one after another in the anticorruption campaign. Among these was Ling Jihua, one of China's mightiest men under Hu Jintao. In the summer of 2012 Ling's twenty-three-year-old son crashed his Ferrari. As described in the previous chapter, the circumstances around this accident angered the Chinese and put the party elite in an unfavorable light. The accident unveiled to the Chinese public the life of luxury, decadence, and irresponsibility of the families of the party elite. In July 2015 Ling was excluded from the party and arrested; a year later he was condemned to life imprisonment for corruption and abuse of power.

Xu Caihou and Guo Boxiong, two top officers under Hu Jintao, suffered similar fates. Xu had been a general and one of three deputy chairmen of the Central Military Commission. In October 2014 he confessed to having accepted huge bribes for promoting officers under his command. When investigators raided his 21,500-square-meter mansion in Beijing, the extent of his corruption became clear. In the cellar they found an Aladdin's cave. It contained more than a ton of cash as well as jade, emeralds, calligraphy, and paintings. It is said that more than ten military lorries were needed to move the plunder.[33] Guo Boxiong had also been a general and deputy chairman of the Central Military Commission, in addition to being a member of the Politburo. Like Xu, he was found guilty of having taken bribes for promoting officers. Brothers in arms, they were both given life sentences.

The networks under these two commanding officers also became the targets of zealous investigators. Former lieutenant general Gu Junshan, one of Xu Caihou's protégés, was among these. At the wedding of Xu's daughter, Gu was so generous that he gave a gift voucher worth $20.6 million or £17.5 million.[34] He could afford it as he had abused his central position in military logistics to make himself rich. From 2009 to 2012 he was second in command of the General Logistics Department of the People's Liberation Army and in charge of the administration of the property of the armed forces. To keep the wheels of the economy going during the financial crisis of 2008, the authorities had started enormous development projects, which also benefitted the military.[35] Developers wanted to secure lucrative contracts, and Gu was far from unbribable. When investigators raided

Gu's home, they seized a mountain of luxury spirits and gold, including a statue of Mao in pure gold worth £8.7 million or $10 million.[36] Investigators also revealed that Gu was about to build a copy of the Forbidden Palace, where Chinese emperors had once lived, in the family's hometown of Puyang in Henan Province, designed by employees of the genuine Forbidden City in Beijing.[37]

This luxury went hand in hand with carnal debaucheries. Voices critical to the government claimed at the start of the twenty-first century, "Behind every corrupt official is a sly mistress." Allegations of a sexual immorality among Tory members of Parliament in the United Kingdom or evangelical preachers in the United States pale in comparison with the hedonism that has developed in elite circles in China, where corruption, money, and mistresses are closely interlinked. Professor Li Yinhe, a prominent Chinese sociologist who has researched sexual behavior, says that the practice of keeping a mistress, in Chinese known as "the second wife" (二奶), reminds one of the practices of the emperors and wealthy men who kept concubines.[38] Concubines were both a source of pleasure and a status symbol. The Communists abolished the practice when they came to power in 1949 (although Mao himself apparently had a constant stream of young women delivered to his bed for years), but it was resurrected in the 1980s hand in hand with the corruption that spread from then on as a result of the economic liberalization Deng Xiaoping initiated. In 2012 a group of researchers at the People's University in Beijing found out that 95 percent of officials in the southern Guangdong Province that were under investigation for corruption kept mistresses.[39] One of these officials, a promiscuous member of the province's land and resources department, was extravagant enough to keep an entire harem of forty-seven mistresses.[40]

Xi realized that the cadres needed a sharp reminder. In January 2013, just two months after his appointment as general secretary of the Chinese Communist Party, you could read the following in an editorial from the official news bureau Xinhua: "As an old Chinese proverb says, there are few heroes who can resist beauty. So, Communist officials should demonstrate the courage of superheroes in the fight against corruption.[41]"

Half of all corruption investigations initiated in Xi's first year were triggered by suspicions of "lifestyle issues," the Chinese media's code word for those who got involved in sex scandals.[42] Little undermines the party's legitimacy more than corrupt officials who misuse public funds to pamper mistresses with presents and luxurious flats.

Undoubtedly, Xi's anticorruption campaign found favor with ordinary Chinese people, and the party propaganda machine has contributed to this approval of Xi's efforts to root out corruption. On March 28, 2017, Hunan Satellite Television, one of China's most popular channels, aired *In the Name of the People*. This series of fifty-five episodes, with roles played by some of China's most celebrated actors, including Lu Yi and Zhang Fengyi, was a smash hit. Hundreds of millions sat in front of their television sets to enjoy this realistic drama about the Disciplinary Commission's hunt for corrupt officials involved in shady property deals in the fictional city of Huanguang in Handong Province. The first episode opens with the police storming into a hotel room, catching a rotten apple in bed with a blonde mistress. Two years before this popular series aired, Hunan Satellite Television had received a directive from the Central Commission for Disciplinary Inspection, instructing the broadcasters to produce more corruption-related films and drama series. *In the Name of the People* came at a highly fortunate moment, only a few months before the Chinese Communist Party would celebrate all that Xi had achieved.

While there was clearly a need to act on corruption and misuse of power, Xi has obviously used the campaign to consolidate his own power, for the purge has been selective.[43] While many members of Jiang Zemin's network and an increasing number of Hu Jintao's have been prosecuted, few of the "princes," the group to which Xi belongs, have. It is true that Bo Xilai, most high-profile of the red aristocracy, fell as a result of charges of corruption and abuse of power, but all of the other "tigers" who were prosecuted had quite ordinary backgrounds, most being descendants of peasants and others of humble origins.[44] One might then suspect that Xi wanted to spare the "princes" from the corruption hunters. The reason for this may be that he has many allies in the red aristocracy or wishes to maintain an image of the descendants of the People's Republic's founders as purer and less corrupt than other groups in Chinese politics. Also, those who have worked closely with Xi in the various stages of his career have remained untouched by the campaign. *ChinaFile*, an online magazine published by the Asia Society, which did a survey of the campaign from 2012 to 2018, has documented that the campaign caught strikingly fewer top officials in the provinces where Xi served for many years, such as Fujian, compared with neighboring provinces.[45]

The anticorruption campaign has without doubt created considerable fear among party cadres. In Xi's second term the campaign has become more institutionalized. Its scope has also broadened to include not just corrupt politicians and officials but also those regarded as incapable of following the party's guidelines or achieving its targets or simply as insufficiently loyal to the party—and Xi.[46] In this way the campaign has become an extremely useful top-down instrument to intimidate the whole party state. No one knows who will next be forced to endure a hell in three acts directed by the Central Commission for Disciplinary Inspection:

Act 1: The committee announces it has opened a case against you.
Act 2: The party dismisses you, if it had not already done so in Act 1, and refers your case to the judicial system for trial.
Act 3: You are on trial and will certainly be found guilty. Then you have to confess on national television, reminding elder viewers of the old Mao days.

Many think suicide is the easiest way out when they hear the committee knock on their door.[47] As Chinese American political scientist Minxin Pei points out, in Xi's China a culture of uncertainty and fear rules in which one tiptoes to avoid falling out of favor with the leader.[48]

## Conclusion

The question we have wrestled with the most to understand Xi's first decade in power, and indeed while working on this book, is how Xi has managed to defy all predictions and achieve such a strong position.

In the specialist literature on the subject there are two hypotheses. The first, which arguably most sinologists support, is that Xi had studied *The Dictator's Handbook* and used all the tricks in the book to seize power at the expense of other leaders and elite networks.[49] He has subdued those around him with the tough personality he developed during his trying youth and with his ability to maneuver to the top. The anticorruption campaign, which more than anything else characterized his first years in power, is the most useful tool he used to discipline his party colleagues. Moreover, Xi's centralization of power swept aside various game rules that had governed elite politics in post-Mao China, such as the principle of collective leadership. This practice had permitted some balance between the various factions within the party. Not least, there was the rule that a leader must retire at seventy and could only sit for two five-year terms. Xi's power consolidation shows that the rules of the game that Deng introduced to regulate Chinese elite politics and prevent a new autocrat were weak as they were poorly institutionalized.[50] In the absence of written rules and procedures, an ambitious leader who spared no means to seize power could easily subdue the entire system. Norms and rules fell like dominos on encountering Xi. Another factor that made Xi's centralization possible was the time at which he became China's leader. Many retired leaders who had previously exerted considerable influence had died or were too old to engage in power politics. Jiang Zemin was eighty-six when Xi came to power, and neither he nor Hu Jintao had any appetite for intrigue. Bo Xilai, Xi's archrival, was out of the frame. His downfall would later drag down China's mighty security tsar, Zhou Yongkang. This left Xi free to steer the ship alone without bothersome rivals.[51]

The second hypothesis, less characterized by drama, intrigue, and power struggle, is that the elite wanted a strong party leader, and the party stood behind Xi in his concentration of power.[52] Prior to the eighteenth party congress, there was a movement within the party from, to use China expert David Shambaugh's concepts, *soft* to *hard authoritarian leaders*. The first group, which had dominated since the end of the 1990s under Jiang Zemin and Hu Jintao, believed that the political system must be opened up. A gradual, controlled opening of the media, education, and civil society could prevent China's Communist regime from becoming history, unlike the Soviet one. Around 2009, just before Xi came to power, the hard authoritarian leaders got the upper hand within the party. The background for this was that Hu and Wen were seen as weak and incapable of coping with a towering mountain of problems facing the party. The hard authoritarians felt the top-down reforms that the softs wanted would be hard to control and would only lead to collapse. The lesson to be learned from Mikhail Gorbachev's attempt to reform the Soviet Union was all too clear. A gradual political opening would spin out of control, and the party would lose its grip. Only enlightened despotism could save the party state, claimed the hards.[53]

On installation, Xi got all three of the key posts. Only a year later, two new superstructures were created, one for reform and one for national security, both with Xi as chairman. At the same time, he was awarded new titles, one after the other, and signs of a personality cult popped up. How could he gain such a prominent position so fast, if not supported by a more or less united elite? As mentioned earlier in this chapter, those appointed by Hu Jintao and Jiang Zemin dominated the Politburo from 2012 to 2017, and only in Xi's next term did Xi's allies form a majority. Why was there so little opposition in the top echelon of the party to Xi's power consolidation?

Of course, a culture of intimidation could deter anyone from expressing any criticism of the leader for fear of reprisal. Nonetheless, a personality cult and an anticorruption campaign are such drastic measures that one might expect more resistance from the other party leaders, especially in the first term. Yes, Jiang was old, Hu was weak, and Bo was out of the picture, but would not other tops, such as Li Keqiang or Wang Yang, associated with Jiang Zemin and Hu Jintao, respectively, have suggested that Xi had taken too much Viagra. Perhaps, instead, they accept Xi's dominant role, thinking that strong centralization of power is necessary as much was at stake for the party state. Perhaps there is a considerable degree of consensus thinking or will to compromise at the top, as well as broad support for removing corrupt politicians and officials who, more than anything, undermine the party's legitimacy. Perhaps Xi does not have such a monopoly of power and is not such a micromanager as he might often appear. Perhaps, instead, he governs like a prime minister who delegates authority and only takes decisions in the most important cases.

We are unable to explain whether the initial concentration of power under Xi was a collective response to the challenges of government or a result of his personal lust for power. Regardless, it is vital to ask the question, as the answer is the key to a fundamental understanding of the dynamics at the top of Xi's China. It can also shed light on whether the dynamics are characterized by a despotic power struggle or rather a more open debate on the challenges faced, a consensus on fundamental ground rules, and cooperation between key political players and networks.

## Notes

1. "China's Xi Allowed to Remain 'President for Life' as Term Limits Removed," BBC News, March 11, 2018.

2. Joseph Fewsmith, "The Sixteenth National Party Congress: The Succession That Didn't Happen," *China Quarterly* 173 (2003): 1–16.

3. See, for example, Graham Allison, "The Chairman of Everything: Why Chinese President Xi Jinping Will Change History," *New Statesman*, December 4, 2017, www.belfercenter.org/publication/chairman-everything-why-chinese-president-xi-jinping-will-change-history; Javier Hernández, "China's 'Chairman of Everything': Behind Xi Jinping's Many Titles," *New York Times*, October 27, 2017; "Chairman of Everything," *The Economist*, April 2, 2016.

4. "Full Text of Resolution on Amendment to CPC Constitution," *China Daily*, October 24, 2017, www.chinadaily.com.cn/china/19thcpcnatinalcogress/2017-10-24/content_3365621_3.htm.

5. Chris Buckley and Steven Lee Myers, "As the West Stumbles, 'Helmsman' Xi Pushes an Ambitious Plan for China," *New York Times*, October 29, 2020.

6. Bill Bostock, "Xi Jinping Could Revive Mao Zedong's Long-Dormant Title of 'Chairman' to Help Him Maintain Total Control, Experts Say," *Business Insider*, August 26, 2020.

7. David Bandurski, "Tracing the 'People's Leader,'" China Media Project, January 21, 2020, https://chinamediaproject.org/2020/01/21/tracing-the-peoples-leader.

8. Qian Gang, "領袖姓名傳播強度觀察" [An observation on the intensity of the transmission of leaders' names], Radio Television Hong Kong, July 11, 2014, http://app3.rthk.hk/mediadigest/content.php?aid=1563.

9. Nectar Gan, "Want to Escape Poverty? Replace Pictures of Jesus with Xi Jinping, Christian Villagers Urged," *South China Morning Post*, November 14, 2017, www.scmp.com/news/china/policies-politics/article/2119699/praise-xi-jinping-not-jesus-escape-poverty-christian.

10. "Xi Jinping Game Show: How Well Do You Know China's Leader?" BBC News, October 4, 2018.

11. Conrad Duncan, "China 'Forces Millions of People' to Download App and Earn Points by Following President Xi Jinping News," *The Independent*, April 8, 2019; Felix Lee, "No One Can Opt Out," *Development and Cooperation*, August 29, 2019, www.dandc.eu/en/article/china-introduces -points-system-rating-social-behaviour; Javier Hernández, "The Hottest App in China Teaches Citizens About Their Leader—and, Yes, There's a Test," *New York Times*, April 7, 2019.

12. Trygve Gulbrandsen, "Eliter," in Sigmund Grønmo, Ann Nilsen, and Karen Christensen (eds.), *Ulikhet: Sosiologiske perspektiver og analyser* [Inequality: sociological perspectives and analyses] (Bergen: Fagbokforlaget, 2021).

13. Neil Thomas, "Ties That Bind: Xi's People on the Politburo," MacroPolo, June 17, 2020, https://macropolo.org/analysis/the-ties-that -bind-xi-people-politburo/; Cheng Li, "Xi Jinping's Inner Circle (Parts 1– 5)," *China Leadership Monitor*, 2014–2015, www.brookings.edu/wp-content /uploads/2016/06/Xi-Jinping-Inner-Circle.pdf.

14. Neil Thomas, "Eye on 2022 (Part 2): Rising Stars in Beijing," MacroPolo, February 16, 2021, https://macropolo.org/ccp-rising-stars-beijing /?rp=e; Willy Lam, "Xi Jinping Raises the Zhejiang Clique, Fights the Communist Youth League," *Asia News*, May 31, 2016, www.asianews.it /news-en/Xi-Jinping-raises-the-Zhejiang-clique,-fights-the-Communist -Youth-League-37642.html.

15. Cheng Li, "Xi Jinping's Inner Circle (Part 2: Friends from Xi's Formative Years)," *China Leadership Monitor*, 2014–2015, www.hoover.org/sites /default/files/research/docs/clm44cl.pdf, 8–10.

16. Cheng, "Inner Circle (Part 2)," 9.

17. Katsuji Nakazawa, "Only Wang Qishan Knew What Xi Jinping Was Going to Do," *Nikkei*, March 26, 2018, https://asia.nikkei.com/Editor-s -Picks/China-up-close/Only-Wang-Qishan-knew-what-Xi-Jinping-was -going-to-do.

18. Cheng, "Inner Circle (Part 2)," 15.

19. Conversations in Hong Kong, October 2018.

20. Conversations in Hong Kong, October 2018.

21. See, for example, Cheng Li, "Wang Huning," Brookings, October 20, 2022, www.brookings.edu/wp-content/uploads/2017/10/china_201710 13_19thpartycongress_wang_huning.pdf; Pratik Jakhar, "China Party Congress: The Rising Stars of China's Communist Party," BBC News, October 8, 2017.

22. Haig Patapan and Yi Wang, "The Hidden Ruler: Wang Huning and the Making of Contemporary China," *Journal of Contemporary China*, 27, no. 109 (2018): 47–60, https://research-repository.griffith.edu.au/bitstream /handle/10072/348664/PatapanPUB3927.pdf.

23. Cheng Li, "Xi Jinping's Inner Circle (Part 5: The Mishu Cluster II)," Brookings Institution, www.brookings.edu/wp-content/uploads/2016/06/China-Leadership-Monitor-Mishu-Cluster-II.pdf.

24. Conversations in Hong Kong, October 2018.

25. Ryan McElveen, "Debunking Misconceptions About Xi Jinping's Anti-corruption Campaign," *China-US Focus*, July 17, 2014, www.chinausfocus.com/political-social-development/debunking-misconceptions-about-xi-jinpings-anti-corruption-campaign; Jonathan Fenby, "China's Corruption Probe Bares Its Teeth," BBC News, February 20, 2015.

26. "Full Text: China's New Party Chief Xi Jinping's Speech," BBC News, November 15, 2012.

27. See, among others, Simon Denyer, "China's Leader, Xi Jinping, Consolidates Power with Crackdowns on Corruption, Internet," *Washington Post*, October 3, 2013; Benjamin Kang Lim and Megha Rajagopalan, "China's Xi Purging Corrupt Officials to Put Own Men in Place: Sources," Reuters, April 17, 2014; Lam, *Chinese Politics*; David Shambaugh, *China's Future* (Cambridge, UK: Polity Press, 2016), 119–120; Christopher Carothers, "Xi's Anti-corruption Campaign: An All-Purpose Governing Tool," *China Leadership Monitor*, March 1, 2021, www.prcleader.org/carothers.

28. "China Punishes More Than 1.5 Million Officials for Corruption," *EFE*, October 19, 2017, www.efe.com/efe/english/world/china-punishes-more-than-1-5-million-officials-for-corruption/50000262-3412841.

29. Tiezzi, "Zhou Yongkang's Greatest Crime."

30. Benjamin Kang Lim and Ken Blanchard, "Exclusive: China Seizes 14.5 Billion Assets from Family, Associates of Ex-Security Chief: Sources," Reuters, March 30, 2013.

31. Conversations in Hong Kong, October 2018; Choi Chi-yuk and Josephine Ma, "Zhou Yongkang, Bo Xilai Among Elite Prisoners in China's 'Tigers' Cage' Qincheng Growing Vegetables and Wearing Suits," *South China Morning Post*, January 13, 2019, www.scmp.com/news/china/politics/article/2181862/elite-prisoners-chinas-tigers-cage-qincheng-grow-vegetables-and.

32. Harrison Jacobs, "Here's the Ridiculous Loot That's Been Found with Corrupt Chinese Officials," *Business Insider*, January 22, 2015.

33. Ma Haoliang, "90多年产生约70名常委 命运各异" [The seventy members of the Politburo's Standing Committee over ninety years—different fates], *Dagong Bao*, March 2, 2015, http://news.takungpao.com/special/szqh_changwei.

34. "揭秘徐才厚谷俊山济南往事" [Revelation of Xu Caihou and Gu Junshan's past in Jinan], *Duowei News*, July 2, 2014, https://article.wn.com/view/WNATde6a4cc4f675f287c169091f6d7d180e.

35. "揭秘徐才厚谷俊山济南往事" [Revelation of Xu Caihou and Gu Junshan's past in Jinan], *Duowei News*.

36. Wang Heyan, "总后副部长谷俊山被查已有两年" [Vice director of PLA's Logistics Deparment, Gu Junshan, has been under investigation for two years], *Shishi Zhongxin*, January 15, 2014.

37. Wang, "总后副部长谷俊山被查已有两年" [Vice Director of PLA's Logistics Department].

38. Li Yinhe interviewed in Chito Romana, "The Return of the Chinese Concubine?" ABC News, September 7, 2009.

39. Tan Jun (ed.), "The Image Crisis of Government Officials in 2012," Renmin University, January 2013. For a summary of the findings of the report, see Zhang Rui, "Statistics: 95% of Corrupted Officials Keep Mistress," China.org.cn, January 9, 2013, www.china.org.cn/china/2013-01/09 /content_27633173.htm.

40. Edward Wong and Mia Li, "Keeping Count: Corrupt Chinese Officials and Their Mistresses," *Sinosphere*, April 27, 2015.

41. "China Feels Women's Weight in Fight Against Graft," *Xinhua*, January 25, 2013, www.china.org.cn/china/2013-01/25/content_27792316 .htm.

42. Elleka Watts, "Prostitution Is Key to Reducing Corruption in China," *The Diplomat*, August 22, 2013.

43. See, among others, Denyer, "China's Leader, Xi Jinping, Consolidates Power"; Lim and Rajagopalan, "China's Xi Purging Corrupt Officials"; Lam, *Chinese Politics*, 105–110; Shambaugh, *China's Future*, 109–120; Carothers, "Xi's Anti-corruption Campaign."

44. See, among others, Shambaugh, *China's Future*, 119–120; Geremie R. Barmé, "Tyger, Tyger—a Fearful Symmetry," *China Story Journal*, October 16, 2014, https://archive.thechinastory.org/2014/10/tyger-tyger-a-fearful -symmetry.

45. "Visualizing China's Anti-corruption Campaign," *ChinaFile*, August 15, 2018, www.chinafile.com/infographics/visualizing-chinas-anti-corruption -campaign.

46. Carothers, "Xi's Anti-corruption Campaign."

47. Nectar Gan, "President Xi Jinping's Corruption Crackdown Linked to Officials' Suicides," *South China Morning Post*, May 3, 2015, www.scmp .com/news/china/policies-politics/article/1784492/president-xi-jinpings -corruption-crackdown-linked.

48. Minxin Pei, "China's Rule of Fear," *Project Syndicate*, February 8, 2015, www.project-syndicate.org/commentary/china-fear-bureaucratic -paralysis-by-minxin-pei-2016-02.

49. For those aspiring to be dictators, see Bruce Bueno de Mesquita, *The Dictator's Handbook: Why Bad Behavior Is Almost Always Good Politics* (New York: PublicAffairs, 2012).

50. Joseph Fewsmith, *Rethinking Chinese Politics* (Cambridge: Cambridge University Press, 2021). For the debate among China observers

about the extent to which Chinese politics is internalized, see Joseph Fewsmith and Andrew J. Nathan, "Authoritarian Resilience Revisited," *Journal of Contemporary China*, September 23, 2018.

51. Brown, *The World According to Xi*, 22.

52. Kerry Brown indicates Xi had the leadership behind him for his centralization of power in "Xi Jinping's Leadership Style: Master or Servant?" *Asian International Studies Review* 17, no. 2 (December 2016): 143–158. The strongest proponent of this view, though, is Nimrod Branovitch, "A Strong Leader for a Time of Crisis: Xi Jinping's Strongman Politics as a Collective Response to Regime Weakness," *Journal of Contemporary China* 30, no. 128 (2021): 249–265.

53. Shambaugh, *China's Future*, chap. 4.

# 4

# Extolling the Leader

ONCE XI JINPING WAS INSTALLED, WE SAW THAT AS A LEADER HE was quite different from his two predecessors. Soon posters of Xi popped up around the capital, showing him in the center of a radiant sun, like the ones of Mao in earlier times or those you might see across the border in North Korea. News of Xi's deeds is all over the front pages. The Chinese sing songs praising Xi Dada and his beautiful wife Peng Mama. Xi's persona is in focus and gets a lot of attention everywhere in the Middle Kingdom. And Xi is given personal credit for any progress China makes. The contrast with the grey, awkward arch-bureaucrat Hu Jintao, whose personal life one scarcely knew anything about, could hardly be greater.

This cult around Xi is a breach of the policy in place since Deng Xiaoping. After Mao Zedong died in 1976 and the dust of the Cultural Revolution had settled, the party elite, headed by Deng, tried their uttermost to avoid the resurrection of a cult of personality and autocratic power. Under Deng, collective leadership—that is, the members of the Politburo's Standing Committee having considerable autonomy within their respective areas of responsibility—was established as a norm for the governance of China. In 1982 Deng had a legal prohibition against personality cults written into the constitution, and Jiang Zemin established formally that he was the first among equals. These laws and norms regulated Chinese politics for thirty years—until Xi came to power.

Why has there arisen a personality cult around China's leader? And to the extent that it is possible to say anything about it, what effect has the cult had?

## China Has Brought Forth a Xi Jinping

The spotlight on Xi has all the characteristics of a personality cult. This cult, which we first saw signs of right after he came to power, is tightly directed by the party propaganda apparatus. This falls under the mighty Publicity Department of the Chinese Communist Party, located in an excellent building near Zhongnanhai at 5 Chang'an Avenue, one of Beijing's main streets. Huang Kunming, one of Xi's most trusted advisors, was head of the department for the first ten years of Xi's reign. Huang has followed Xi through most of the latter's career, and the two worked together in the provinces of Fujian and Zhejiang among other places. The year after Xi became the Chinese Communist Party's general secretary, Huang was appointed to a leading position in the Publicity Department, which he headed until October 2022. So it was he who got the job of directing the Xi cult. As mentioned several times, Xi keeps his cards close to his chest, so the Chinese people know little about him. This has produced a mystical aura about the man, which is a good start for a cult of personality. Since people know so little, Huang and the propaganda unit are pretty much free to paint Xi as almost divine without any disturbing known facts to contradict this.

Xavier Márquez, a researcher on authoritarian rulers, provides a useful analytical framework for understanding personality cults around political leaders. He believes that such cults can be conceptualized in two separate ways, as propaganda that depicts the leader favorably and as rituals expressing support and worship for the leader.

Propaganda is information that powerful agents produce and spread with the aim of changing or influencing the opinions of large groups of people. Propaganda therefore distinguishes itself from other forms of communication by its sheer volume, giving the leader

an unusually high and positive status and even granting him exceptional and superhuman abilities.[1]

Official communication about Xi in Chinese media has all these
characteristics. The volume of information and attention is extraordinarily large. The *People's Daily*—the Chinese Communist Party's
own and one of China's most read newspapers—gives Xi lots of column inches. A comparative study of the number of articles devoted
to the general secretary in his first eighteen months in power shows
that Xi got more than double the number his predecessors got. Xi
was mentioned 4,725 times, while Hu and Jiang got respectively
2,405 and 2,001 mentions. If you look at the number of articles on
the first eight pages that mention the general secretary by name, the
difference is also clear. Xi is named in twice as many articles as Jiang
and Hu—4,186 against Jiang's 1,987 and Hu's 1,993.[2]

Other media also contribute to the personality cult. Hunan TV is
one of the most popular channels in China, with the young population
as its target group. For a period, it aired a game show called *Study Xi*
about his life and ideology. The program was in the same lavish, modern, colorful style as Saturday night quiz programs on British or
American TV, aired in prime time with live studio audiences. Participants were asked about Xi's ideology and personal life—for instance,
which book Xi had walked fifteen kilometers to collect when he lived
in Liangjiahe during the Cultural Revolution—or they were asked to
complete sentences from his public speeches.[3]

The propaganda apparatus has also embraced modern media in
its marketing of Xi.[4] The *People's Daily* has started a virtual fan club,
the Group for the Study of Xi, which is different from other official
and news channels in that it exclusively publishes articles about Xi;
his travels, speeches, and statements.[5]

In addition to the country's media, Chinese academia plays a key
role in cultivating Xi and is therefore among the powerful agents
Márquez includes in his definition of propaganda. For example,
research on Xi's thought is given priority within the social sciences
and philosophy. During Hu Jintao's ten years in office, the National
Social Science Fund awarded funding to 15.5 projects with Hu Jintao
in the title per year.[6] Xi, in contrast, so far has 48.6 projects named

after him annually. In June 2018 the Shaanxi Academy of Social Science announced research funding for projects about "Liangjiahe's magnificent teaching" (梁家河大学问), with reference to the decade Xi spent in his youth in the countryside during the Cultural Revolution.[7] The expressed aim was to promote insight into why Xi has become the party core, commander in chief of the armed forces, and the leader of the people, as well as into Xi's thoughts about "socialism with Chinese characteristics for a new era."[8] Three of the most popular research themes in 2018 were linked to Xi's thoughts.[9] A year earlier it was announced that ten centers for research on "Xi Jinping's socialism with Chinese characteristics for a new era" would be opened at Chinese universities.[10]

Not only is the amount of material on Xi unusually big, but it is also unusually positive. In many cases party representatives spread it, in the same way that "leadership clans" customarily contribute to the process of producing a charismatic leader.[11] One example is a series of articles published by the Central Party School in spring 2018 about the positive response Xi had gotten in the foreign media. The title of the first article sets the tone for the entire series: "Extraordinary Leader: A Study of the International Praise for the Super Strong Leadership of Xi Jinping in the New Era."[12] Another example is an article by General Liu Yazhou from 2014 describing Xi's book *The Governance of China* as "an ideological torch that lights up the Chinese dream."[13]

The Chinese dream is at the heart of the Xi propaganda and an example of his being ascribed exceptional qualities and given personal honor for the great progress China has made or is making. One aim of the dream is that China should become a *moderately prosperous* country, that the Chinese should no longer be poor; another is that the Chinese nation should *rejuvenate* and once again become a great power. Xi presented this dream straight after his inauguration; it soon became his motto and is therefore closely associated with him. As the two are so closely linked, the impression is created that Xi personally is the guarantor that China will never again suffer a century of humiliation, that it will rise once more and regain its rightful international position.

This message is brought to the people on a massive scale, on billboards, in the media, and even in people's homes in the form of calendars. The most important holiday for the Chinese is the Chinese new year. It is rather like Christmas for Westerners, a time to visit family and exchange presents. Calendars for the New Year are common gifts. When we entered the Year of the Sheep in 2015, calendars with photos of Xi were decidedly the most popular: Xi with rockets, with the first hangar ship, or with Peng Mama, often with the caption "The Chinese Dream" in gold. The message of Xi's strength and excellence thereby entered people's homes and stayed with them for the whole year in the same way that pictures and statues of Mao did in his time. An important characteristic of a personality cult, according to Yin Liangen and Terry Flew, is just that: symbols linked to the leader find their way into ordinary people's lives.[14]

There is nothing new about the Chinese Communist Party spreading the good news about the country's positive development. What is new is that Xi personally is given credit for it, something not seen since Mao. In autumn 2017 the exhibition *After Five Years* opened at Beijing's exhibition center. It was to show the progress the nation had made under the Xi administration's first term. The exhibition was, however, exclusively about Xi. In the section on China's military progress, for instance, there were all of twenty-four giant pictures of Xi. Several of the exhibits clearly had more to do with Xi as a person than with the country's development—for example, a photo of Xi stroking a baby elephant, a football shirt presented to Xi by Pelé, and souvenirs from a visit to Liangjiahe, the village where he lived during the Cultural Revolution, such as embroideries and a photo of a receipt for a meal.[15]

There are innumerable other examples of the spotlight being trained on Xi's personal life. For a time, he was called Xi Dada, which can be translated as "daddy," "uncle," or "big brother" Xi. This nickname probably has two purposes. First, it emphasizes his closeness to and care for the people. Second, it alludes to Confucian ideas of hierarchy. Everyone should conduct themselves in accordance with their status in society; children should obey and respect their elders and parents and subjects, their rulers. In return, superiors owe their inferiors care and attention. The nickname Xi Dada reminds the people of their obligations to Xi as well as the respect they owe him.

Songs and poems about Xi as a private person flourish like those about Mao did in his time. His relations with his wife, Peng Liyuan, form the theme of songs in a way that is quite new in Chinese history. Known examples are "If you are going to get married, marry a man like big brother Xi," "Xi Dada loves Peng Mama," and to the delight of the kids, "Grandad Xi is our big friend."[16] There is even a comic strip about Xi's interest in soccer.[17] Mao too waded in rivers of songs and poems composed in his praise, but they had far less intimate themes. Consider the words of the song "Xi Dada Loves Peng Mama" (习大大爱着彭麻麻) (our translation):

China has a Xi Dada.
No matter how strong the tiger is he dares fight him.
He is fearless,
People die to meet him, even in their dreams.
China also has a Peng Mama,
Give her the most beautiful flowers.
Pray for her and bless her.
Happy family, flourishing country, harmonious world
Xi Dada loves Peng Mama
Their love is legendary.
Peng Mama loves Xi Dada,
The kingdom with love is the strongest
Men should learn from Xi Dada,
Women should learn from Peng Mama
Love like they do.
Love can warm thousands of families.
. . .
People with love can win the world!
This is the type of love Xi Dada gives Peng Mama.
When they are together,
He always looks at her with a gentle smile.
. . .
While holding his hand, her smile is the most beautiful flower.

Songs of praise can also be found in less personal variants, such as the new version of "The East Is Red" (东方红). Originally in praise of Mao and highly popular during the Cultural Revolution, the lyrics went "The East is red / The sun has risen / China has brought forth a Mao Zedong." In the new version Mao's name has been replaced with that of Xi. Another example is a poem one of the directors of the news agency Xinhua wrote in 2018 and published on the internet. It starts,

> General Secretary, your back and my gaze.
> My eyes are giving birth to this poem.
> My fingers are burning on my cellphone.

After three hours the poem had been read by 20,000 people, and it continued to spread like wildfire in dry grass.[18]

The point of focusing so strongly on Xi as a person is to make people feel they have a special bond with him. Such a personal bond is a characteristic of charismatic leadership and, according to American political sociologist Ronald M. Glassman, gives individuals full confidence and an irrational faith in their leader, accepting whatever he does.[19]

Some presentations of Xi emphasize that he is a quite normal man. He is presented as a man not just *for* the people but also *of* the people. One instance is when he visited the village he lived in during the Cultural Revolution. When meeting his old friends, they were at first rather stiff and quiet, unsure how to behave with the nation's leader. But Xi soon broke the ice by telling an old friend that he had put on weight.[20] Jovial and down to earth!

At numerous public appearances, Xi has been presented as someone who cares for and is one of the people. When, as a fresh president, he visited fishermen on the island of Hainan, state media reported how he chatted with them and asked about their everyday lives and life at sea.[21] Another example that probably went according to plan and got lots of attention was when, in December 2013, he popped into a simple dumpling shop on Beijing's west side. He behaved like an ordinary customer, queuing up like everyone else, paying from his own pocket, and carrying his own tray with the simple meal to one of the cheap, foldable tables in the spartan premises.[22] Those who thought Xi was an establishment figure who only ate at extravagant banquets had to think again. Xi could feel just as much at home in simple cheap joints where most people eat. He gorged himself on simple dumplings. The event reminds us of when King Olav of Norway took a tram during the 1973 petrol crisis, left his car in the garage, and gave his chauffeur a day off, insisting on paying for his own ticket.

## Clap, Dance, and Study Xi!

Somewhat less visible than the propaganda but just as much part of the personality cult are the rituals that express worship of or reverence for Xi. According to Xavier Márquez, a ritual is any practice that involves a group of people acting together to focus on a special object or symbol and sharing an understanding of what they are focusing on. A ritual need not be formal or ceremonial. Nor do the participants need to act together completely, as rituals can be communicated in other ways than physical presence—for example, through television broadcasting.[23]

We can find several examples of such rituals in Xi's China. We previously mentioned in this chapter how songs were composed in praise of the nation's great leader. These spread, and people learn them, as well as the dance steps that in some cases go with the songs, by heart. They then gather to sing and dance them in public.

In the digital domain, too, we find rituals praising Xi, but here participants do not necessarily know about each other. The Chinese IT company Tencent, China's most valuable company, created the mobile app "Clap for Xi Jinping" during the 2017 party congress. In this app users can give virtual applause to Xi's speeches by pushing the applause button as many times as they can within eighteen seconds and then share the results with other participants and compete with friends. In a flash the app had been used more than a billion times.[24] While people had many opportunities to clap for Mao at mass rallies during the Cultural Revolution, the opportunities to clap for Xi are for most limited to the virtual sphere.

Another mobile app, with a name that can translate to either "Study to Strengthen the Country" or "Study Xi to Strengthen the Country" (学习强国), awards points to those who read speeches, watch videos, and participate in quizzes about Xi. The app is thus a modern-day digital equivalent of both *Quotations from Chairman Mao* (*Mao's Little Red Book*) and study circles of the book; the purpose is to spread knowledge of the leader and his policies among the population at large. Many employees in state institutions are evaluated according to how many points they accumulate, and they risk a reprimand if they do not fulfil minimum requirements. The points accumulated can be used in selected shops, where they can be exchanged for small gifts, discounts, or free tickets.[25]

A final example of the personal cult in cyber space is the expression "long live" (万岁), which during imperial times was used to greet the emperor whenever he left the palace. While Mao efficiently scrapped many remnants of imperial times, this was a custom he gladly retained. Mao's Red Guards frequently shouted, "Long live Mao!" during mass gatherings. After him no Chinese leader allowed use of the phrase until Xi. It can now be found on blogs and banners hung in public.[26]

Some of the rituals for the cultivation of Xi have a religious flavor, as is often the case with such cults.[27] For example, people go on pilgrimage to Liangjiahe, the village Xi stayed in during the Cultural Revolution.[28] A tree Xi planted in 2009 in Lankao in Henan Province has become an icon party cadres visit to express their loyalty to Xi and to get inspiration and political education.[29] Local media has described the tree in this way: "Like a bright red flag, it instructs the masses of party members to not forget the mission, to stay the path and forge ahead."[30] When Xi visited the city of Chaozhou in Guangdong in October 2020, a middle-aged woman aroused attention when she held her hands pressed together in front of her in the gesture the Chinese use when praying to the gods in sacred places.[31] During the same trip Xi visited Shantou. Afterward a gold brick was laid down in the street where he had given his speech, bearing with the date and time of the event.[32] Since then local authorities have arranged frequent activities there and at the park he visited, for team building and inspiration.[33]

A typical religious element of the type "thou shalt have no other gods but me" can also be traced in the Xi cult. Christian churches and Buddhist temples and even private homes have sometimes had to replace their religious imagery and symbols with pictures of Xi.[34] In a village in Jiangxi Province, the local Catholic church had to swap its picture of the Virgin Mary and the Baby Jesus, hung in the most prominent place in the church, with a large portrait of Xi. In Yugan County a total of 624 Christian pictures and quotations were taken down and replaced with pictures of Xi.[35] Local officials also visited Christian homes with posters of Xi and asked the inhabitants to switch any pictures of Jesus they had hanging with the posters and Xi quotations. In a small town in Henan Province, churches had to exchange posters of the Ten Commandments with posters of Xi's quotations.[36]

Even if people's daily lives are less characterized by activities lauding their leader today than under Mao, this phenomenon is something new, as such worship was completely absent under Xi's two predecessors, Jiang and Hu. Zhang Lifan, a historian at China's Academy of Social Sciences, has described the cult around Xi as "a new round of the god-creation movement, similar to the Mao era."[37]

Rituals have a stronger effect than propaganda on the individual, according to Márquez, because the feeling of obligation to the leader is strengthened when one participates actively.[38] One example is the applause app described above. The speeches you could clap for were often about the measures Xi had taken to help and protect the weakest.[39] The effect of propaganda about Xi as a strong and caring leader is magnified by people expressing their individual support for this message. David Bandurski, director of the China Media Project at the University of Hong Kong, emphasizes the strong effect of the app: "It is really revolutionary in the sense that it induces people to participate in an act of adulation. The individual becomes a part of propaganda—and even, potentially, enjoys the experience."[40] William Callahan, professor at the London School of Economics and expert on Chinese politics, interprets rituals such as these as a way for the authorities to build legitimacy and to exert censorship and control: "It encourages and feeds off popular feelings and mass action, much like the Cultural Revolution of Mao Zedong in 1966."[41]

## A Strong Leader After a Lost Decade

It is striking that the Xi personality cult arose right after he took over as general secretary of China's Communist Part in 2012. It is hard to imagine that Xi's position would have been strong enough for him to singlehandedly get such a cult going without stirring up trouble among the other leaders. That it all began so swiftly and so strongly right after the power shift indicates that the party elite had planned it in advance. This supports the idea that the power Xi has today is something not that he has snatched but that a united elite has willingly granted him, as suggested in the preceding chapter.

As described in Chapter 2, at the end of the Hu Jintao era, the Chinese Communist Party faced huge challenges. There was broad agreement about the need for a stronger leader to tackle these problems—one who could create enthusiasm for the party. Hu's authority had been based purely on his formal positions, what Max Weber called *rational-legal authority*, where people's ties to the leader are impersonal ties to an office. Little in his personality or curriculum vitae gave any foundation for any other type of authority.

Mao and Deng, on the other hand, had an excess of *charismatic authority*, or authority based on the people's belief in a specific person's extraordinary qualities.[42] Both had played decisive roles in saving the country from external occupants and internal enemies and established the People's Republic; thus, they are typical examples of historic actors with the aura of successful military leaders and state builders.[43] Their charismatic authority was far more important than their formal positions. In practice, Deng led China from 1976 until his death in 1997, despite never being either general secretary or president. His highest post was chairman of the Military Commission from 1981 to 1989. After that his only formal position was leader of the National Bridge Association. Nonetheless, no one was ever in doubt about who was boss and had the last word.

Xi's authority is a mixture of rational-legal and charismatic. All three of China's most powerful posts—general secretary of the party, chairman of the Central Military Commission, and president of China—were served to him on a silver platter. In addition, he began to collect a heap of other titles at the same time as the party elite started building a cult of personality around him. The fact that during his first eighteen months in power the *People's Daily* had already given him twice as many column inches as they had given to Hu is an example of this. Probably the party elite thought the authority of the supreme leader had to be based both on formal positions and charisma. They had experienced how the type of authority Hu had was nowhere near adequate to either govern the country or create enthusiasm. Therefore, they had in all likelihood decided to build a personality cult around Xi even before he came to power.[44] Nonetheless, his charismatic authority is too weak to work on its own, and Xi's power is dependent on his formal positions. China expert Kerry Brown compares Mao's position with that of Xi in this way: While Mao could defy and challenge the party during the Cultural Revolution because his personal power was independent of the party, this is unthinkable for Xi. He is powerful because the party he leads is powerful and he has no individual power outside the party.[45]

The cult of personality fulfils several purposes. The most important is to strengthen the position and therefore the *legitimacy* of Xi among the population and, thereby, the party's monopoly on power.[46] Another aim is to contribute to *social integration and cohesiveness*.[47] Earlier this chapter described a number of Xi-centered rituals. Joint participation in just such rituals enhances feelings of belonging, according to Márquez. In a country of 1.4 billion people, fifty-six ethnic groups, huge cultural, economic, and geographic differences, and, at times, considerable dissatisfaction, a cult of personality may be one way of dealing with the forces that might pull the country apart. China is a good example of a large-scale society that has such big problems of cohesion that it finds having a charismatic (*irrational*) symbol of unity necessary to deal with them, as Glassman puts it.[48]

Similarly, the *Chinese dream* seeks to create integration in Chinese society by acting as "social glue." It does this by exploiting history, culture, and patriotism.[49] Social instability has raised the question of what it means to be Chinese; the Chinese dream was created to construct a Chinese national identity.[50]

A third aim of the cult is probably to arouse *enthusiasm* for Xi and the party. The Chinese dream, Xi's signature project, seems designed to rally the people. The authorities have left the dream vague, which means that the concept can embrace transcendental content and goals that are above, bigger, more important, longer lasting, and beyond the everyday and worldly: "the Chinese people's magnificent rejuvenation" (中华民 族伟大复兴).[51] This narrative is made to create enthusiasm, what Émile Durkheim calls *collective effervescence*.[52] Glassman maintains a corresponding effect of charismatic leadership that he calls *morale boosting*.[53] So the dream has the same function as charismatic leadership, which is to represent the hope and values of a group.[54]

Since the authorities have left the dream vague, the Chinese are free to fill it with their own meaning. Posters about the dream often say as much: "The Chinese dream—my dream!" Clearly the aim is to create a personal bond between the people and the dream and, with it, between them and Xi and the party. In telling stories about people who have been motivated by the dream to work for their own personal objectives, the media show that the dream can contribute toward meaning and purpose for the individual.[55] In this way the dream may fulfil two of the functions Durkheim gives religion—creating social coherence and giving meaning and purpose.

## A New Mao Cult?

For many the Xi cult prompts memories of the Mao cult during the Cultural Revolution—and not without reason. *Mao's Little Red Book*, which Chinese always kept in their inner pocket in the 1960s and 1970s, has been replaced by the mobile app "Study Xi to Strengthen the Country." Once again, everyone has to study the leader's writing on a regular basis. Xi has also resurrected the tradition of self-criticism meetings, which were widespread in Mao's time—sessions that seem more a general preventive than a matter of reeducation.

Xi, like Mao, is not content with occupying people's minds; bodies have to be engaged to prove both that people are loyal and that they have internalized obedience to the leader. Under Mao they danced "the loyalty dance" (忠字舞), a collective activity where they danced, sang, jumped, and shouted to rousing music with *Mao's Little Red Book* in their hands. Participating in the dance was often obligatory, and even grandmothers with bound feet were not excused.[56] Today in parks and market squares we can come across Chinese singing and dancing their praise of Xi.

The country's newspaper editors rarely need to wonder what to put on the front page tomorrow—as with Mao, Xi's every movement will get fat banner headlines. While much time was devoted to Mao on the radio, Xi is given as much viewing time on television, often with enthusiastic supporters applauding remarkably loud and long.

And those who do not read papers or watch TV will see Xi on posters in parks and along the roads as the previous generation saw Mao. In Mao's time, statues of the great leader were never far apart. Those outdoors had to be exactly 7.1 meters tall to mark the date the Communist Party was founded, July 1, 1921. Mao statues of smaller size were common property. Xi too has found his way into people's homes. Admittedly, you will have to search for some time to find a statue of Xi, but posters, calendars, tea sets, and plates bearing Xi's face are readily available. As we have said, it is popular to make a pilgrimage to Xi's cave from the Cultural Revolution, just as it is to visit Mao's childhood home in the village of Shaoshan in Hunan Province.

Even if many aspects of the two cults are the same, the aims are different. For Xi the main object is to arouse enthusiasm and support for the Chinese Communist Party, and the party is behind the cult. It was quite different with the Mao cult, where the assault on the party bureaucracy was central. Mao started the cult because he was unsure of the support of the rest of the party leaders. He therefore wanted to secure direct, personal support from the people. Xi aims to secure support for himself as well as for the party, via his own personage, whereas Mao sought support for himself outside and independent of the party. Mao felt he relied on popular support because he lacked support within the party. Xi's power, on the other hand, is dependent on the party. The popular blogger Ren Yi, son of the 1980s reformists, thinks that Mao's Cultural Revolution has much in common with Donald Trump's urging his supporters to fight the result of the 2020 presidential election, which led them to storm Capitol Hill.[57]

The Xi cult can be seen as belonging to a historical tradition of worshipping leaders in China and the rest of East Asia, which precedes Mao. The attention given to Xi today harkens back to imperial times when the emperor was looked on as "the son of heaven" and had a "mandate from heaven" to rule the Middle Kingdom. This system of government was founded on two philosophical schools that have set their mark on Chinese society to this day, Confucianism, which emphasizes a hierarchical social order with the emperor at the top, and legalism, which emphasizes the importance of the ruler having tight control over the administration and population and holds autocracy as its ideal. Of course, the rhetoric around the power position of the top leaders has changed since imperial times, but the underlying principles remain the same.

Indeed, Xi seems to hold a position closer to "the mandate from heaven" than did his predecessors. This grants the ruler the right to govern unopposed, as long as he (with one exception around the turn of the 7th century China has never had a woman head of state) fulfils certain conditions. The Chinese expect the ruler to be all powerful and full of care for his subjects. He is expected to ensure economic prosperity, stability, and security for citizens and glory for a strong and powerful country. Much of the propaganda we have described earlier in this chapter aims to communicate that Xi fulfils these conditions and is therefore a rightful ruler.

## Conclusion

Does the personality cult work? Do the Chinese buy it? Measuring the effect of a propaganda campaign is always hard, and in a country such as China, almost impossible. All the same, there is reason to believe that several aspects of the Chinese dream resonate with large sectors of the Chinese population, not least those concerning China's international position.

Nationalism is a powerful force in Chinese society, resulting from, among other things, the extensive nationalistic campaign the Chinese Communist Party has carried out since the 1990s to strengthen its legitimacy. This nationalism is grounded in the idea of a century of humiliation alongside pride in both past glories and current economic expansion. After decades of cautious foreign policy, characterized by Deng's defensive line, the rhetoric about China's reassuming its rightful global place resonates well with the Chinese. So, from all accounts, Xi's assertive international profile is winning their support. Ordinary people appreciate that Xi is a strong leader who gets things done. He is someone they can be proud of.[58] As Wang Feng, a forty-five-year-old mid-level civil servant, puts it, "Our president has a stiff spine and will lead China to a brighter place."[59]

Chinese traditional values also favor the personality cult. It fits in well with Confucian ideals about the relationship between ruler and subject. Xi's nickname, Xi Dada, fits in with the traditional idea of good governance, where the head of state is like a father to his people: he is responsible for their welfare, sympathizes with their needs, and takes care of them.[60] In imperial times the expression "parental officials" (父母官) was used to express this obligation.[61] Xi presents himself as someone who takes this obligation very seriously, as a ruler who governs with wisdom, compassion, and a deep devotion to his people and feels responsible for doing right by them and guiding them.[62] Similarly, Lucian Pye, political scientist and sinologist, claims that the Chinese want a leader who can solve all their problems.[63] Even if one can sweep aside such claims as orientalist generalizations, it does seem that traditional values paves the way for "a personality cult to be effective in China. This would be in accordance with Glassman's thesis that charismatic authority works best when the group governed feel a personal, trust-based, and infantilizing bond to the leader.[64]

Such a view of what constitutes a good leader is widespread in China. This is confirmed by studies. Andrew J. Nathan, China specialist and professor at Columbia University in New York, carried out big surveys over several years in various Asian countries to map political culture and values. Among the questions he asked were to what degree respondents agreed with the statement "Government leaders are like the head of a family; we should all follow their decisions." In the People's Republic of China, 68 percent agreed, while only 23 percent agreed in Taiwan.[65] This was one of nine questions all connected to what Nathan calls traditional social values: conflict shyness, obedience to authorities, and group loyalty. 64 percent of Chinese in the People's Republic said they agreed with these values indicating how widespread they are there. Nathan believes that the Chinese culture and traditional values are a main reason why such a large portion supports the authorities.[66] They may also be also why the personality cult resonates so well with the Chinese people.

Even though much of the content of the cult is suitable to engage support—and probably work—in large sectors of the population, we see signs that not all buy the propaganda about Xi. His folksy lunch in a dumpling bar, for instance, was at first well received, but after a few weeks, "dumpling" (包子) became a symbol in protest actions against inequality and injustice.[67] The huge attention given to the dumpling meal and Liangjiahe, the village where Xi lived for several years during the Cultural Revolution, has been ridiculed in the social media: "A business suggestion . . . Liangjiahe dumplings could be sold all over the world, in theory it could also be sold to other planets," wrote a sarcastic Twitter user.[68] After gold bricks were laid in the streets of Shantou, where Xi had stood during his visit there, several netizens reacted, pointing out that it reminded them of imperial times. With reference to Xi's dumpling meal, Xi got the nickname "the dumpling emperor."[69]

The quiz show about Xi on Hunan TV unleashed several remarks ridiculing it on Weibo, China's Twitter: "Anyone who had wrong answer should be reeducated to meet the requirement in the new era," wrote one user, lashing out at both China's system for "reeducating" political dissidents and Xi's most famous slogan, "Socialism with Chinese characteristics for a new era."[70]

The clap app has also been used to express political opposition, if more subtly. Twenty-eight-year-old engineer Yang Kaiwen played twice, making sure to clap exactly 404 times on each occasion, and posted these results online. The number was a reference to error messages of the type "404 not found," a hint at China's internet censorship.[71]

Márquez asserts that propaganda that is perceived as unbelievable or ridiculous will either not have the desired effect or have a limited effect.[72] Indeed, the Chinese authorities may be thinking along these lines, for since 2018 some of the expressions of the personality cult have been toned down.[73] For example, in July 2018 the central authorities prohibited local authorities from hanging up posters of Xi without obtaining prior permission from Beijing.[74] Clearly, the Xi Dada campaign went too far, and the media have been told not to use the nickname.[75] One reason is probably that the name was an object of sarcasm and ridicule, which are hardy and dangerous forms of criticism. Another reason may be that the image of a kind and caring ruler clashes with another, just as important ideal, that of the strong leader.

Therefore, since 2018, the Chinese authorities have to some extent tried to limit or counteract certain types of expression of the personality cult that can simply be contradicted or are obviously exaggerated; propaganda only lends legitimacy to the regime if bought into and internalized by a sufficient part of the population. For the Chinese political elite there is an additional aspect that arouses special concern that the cult may go too far. If it resembles the Mao cult too much, there is the danger that it may reopen the wounds of the Cultural Revolution, which are still sore for many Chinese, and create negative reactions among the population. The strong link between Xi and the party means his popularity benefits the party. But the opposite can also happen. Opposition to Xi and the Xi cult can work against the party.

It is hard to know how much of the propaganda people genuinely believe in. Nonetheless, it serves a useful purpose for Xi and the party. The most vital point of the propaganda in a personality cult is compliance, not necessarily genuine support from the population.[76] The aim might not be to convince the recipient of the message but to communicate how she or he is expected to relate to the leader, especially in terms of expressions of support.

Such an effect can be enhanced by people gathering to participate in rituals as well as receiving propaganda. Participation can strengthen motivation for *conformity*, for following guidelines, even among those who do not feel especially attracted to the leader.[77] Just such a dynamic seems to be what the Hong Kong newspaper the *Apple Daily* (shut down on June 23, 2021, after pressure from Beijing) described among local authorities: only doing what all others do, knowing that the leader wishes and demands their praise, in order to gain political security and promotion at a low cost.[78]

Even when the effect of a personality cult is merely conformity, the authorities obtain the desired effect, not then having to use so much force and coercion to get the population to behave as they want.[79] Sinologist and historian Frank Dikötter put it this way:

"When you see the underlings of a leader enthusiastically applaud, you should feel fear. Because that's precisely what they feel."[80]

## Notes

1. See Xavier Márquez, "Two Models of Political Leader Cults: Propaganda and Ritual," *Politics, Religion & Ideology* 19, no. 3 (2018): 268.

2. Qian, "領袖姓名" [An observation on the intensity].

3. "Xi Jinping Game Show," BBC News.

4. Tyler Lynch, "China Has Brought Forth a Xi Dada: How China Is Making and Breaking the Personality Cult of Xi Jinping," *Undergraduate Journal of Politics, Policy and Society* 3, no. 1 (2020): 77–89, www.ujpps.com /index.php/ujpps/article/view/71.

5. "学习小组" [Group for Studies of Xi], *Baidu*, https://baike.baidu .com/item/%E5%AD%A6%E4%B9%A0%E5%B0%8F%E7%BB%84.

6. Neil Thomas, "More Money for Marxism in China's Social Science Research," MacroPolo, November 30, 2020, https://macropolo.org/china -marxist-ideology-research-funding/?rp=m.

7. See, for example, "在梁家河感受'大学问'" [To experience magnificent teaching in Liangjiahe], CPC News, June 20, 2018, http://cpc.people .com.cn/n1/2018/0620/c64387-30069245.html.

8. Screendump printed in David Bandurski, "Researching China's Sacred Leader," China Media Project, June 20, 2018, https://chinamedia project.org/2018/06/27/the-social-science-of-sacred-leadership.

9. "2017年度中国十大学术热点" [China's ten academic hotspots in 2017], CPC News, January 17, 2018, http://theory.people.com.cn/n1/2018 /0117/c40531-29770391.html.

10. "中央批准的10家习近平新时代中国特色社会主义思想研究中心（院）相继成立" [The ten research centres on Xi Jinping's thoughts on socialism with Chinese characteristics for a new era that the central authorities have accepted are being established the one after the other], CPC News, April 18, 2018, http://theory.people.com.cn/n1/2018/0418/c 40531-29932832.html.

11. See p. 624 in Ronald Glassman, "Legitimacy and Manufactured Charisma," *Social Research* 42, no. 4 (1975): 615–636.

12. "了不起的领导人—习近平新时代超强领导力国际赞誉研究" [Research on international praise of Xi Jinping's superstrong leadership in the new era], China Media Project, June 2018, https://chinamediaproject .org/wp-content/uploads/2018/06/了不起的领导人_习近平新时代超强领导力国际赞誉研究_本刊编辑部-1.pdf.

13. Liu Yazhou, "照耀中国梦的思想火炬" [An ideological torch shining on the Chinese dream], *Renmin ribao*, February 4, 2015, http://politics.people.com.cn/n/2015/0204/c1001-26502540.html.

14. Yin Liangen and Terry Flew, "Xi Dada Loves Peng Mama—Digital Culture and the Return of Charismatic Authority in China," *Thesis Eleven* 144, no. 1 (2018): 80–99.

15. "Xi's Menus Revealed at Exhibition," *China Daily*, September 30, 2017, www.chinadaily.com.cn/china/2017-09/30/content_32676573_2.htm; Tom Phillips, "All-Conquering Xi: China Hails Its Leader in Ecstatic Beijing Exhibition," The Guardian, October 9, 2017.

16. Bo Zhiyue, "In China, an Ode to 'Grandpa Xi,'" *The Diplomat*, June 17, 2015, https://thediplomat.com/2015/06/in-china-an-ode-to-grandpa-xi.

17. "网友原创'习大大与足球'萌系画风赢点赞" [The sweet style in "Xi Dada and football" reaps praise], *Renmin ribao*, July 2, 2014, http://culture.people.com.cn/n/2014/0702/c22219-25229315.html.

18. Hannah Beech, "Ode to Autocracy: Viral Poem Highlights Cult of China's Leader," *Time Magazine*, February 19, 2016.

19. Glassman, "Legitimacy and Manufactured Charisma," 624.

20. Anonymous, *Liangjiahe Village*, 28.

21. An Baijie, "President Pays Visit to Hainan Fishermen," *China Daily*, April 11, 2013.

22. Sun Chaoyi, "习总书记排队点餐取餐全程自己来" [General Secretary Xi queued up, ordered food, paid, and did everything himself], *Zhongguo Gongchandang xinwen*, December 29, 2012, www.scmp.com/news/china/article/1392160/president-xi-buys-meal-beijing-bun-shop.

23. Márquez, "Two Models of Political Leader Cults," 275–276.

24. "Players 'Applaud' Xi Jinping in Tencent Game," BBC News, October 20, 2017.

25. Audrey Jiajia Li, "Uber but for Xi Jinping," *New York Times*, April 4, 2019; Michael Keane and Su Guanhua, "When Push Comes to Nudge: A Chinese Digital Civilisation in-the-Making," *Media International Australia* 173, no. 1 (2019): 3–16; Hernández, "The Hottest App in China Teaches Citizens About Their Leader"; "How Xi Jinping Became God," *Bitter Winter*, January 1, 2020.

26. Yin and Flew, "Xi Dada Loves Peng Mama," 30–31; *New Highland Vision*, 海风：有人终于喊出了习近平万岁，这也是预料之中的结果 [Someone finally called out Long Live Xi Jinping, this is the expected result], *Twitter*, https://twitter.com/5xyxh/status/1142852310441320449.

27. See, for example, Thomas A. Wright and Tyler L. Lauer, "What Is Character and Why It Really Does Matter," *Organizational Dynamics* 42 (2013): 25–34; Yin and Flew, "Xi Dada Loves Peng Mama," 9–12.

28. Andrew Jacobs and Chris Buckley, "Move Over Mao: Beloved 'Papa Xi' Awes China," *New York Times*, March 7, 2015.

29. "谢伏瞻和省委常委集体瞻仰'焦桐'、凝望'习桐'" [Xie Fuzhan and the province committee's standing committee praise together "Jiao tong" and gaze at "Xi tong"]. *Henan ribao*, November 8, 2017, www.henandaily.cn/content/zhengwu/hnsfl/jgcy/2017/1108/74615.html; Viola Zhou, "Chinese Officials Pay Homage to Tree Planted by Xi Jinping as Communist Party Chiefs Get in Touch with Their Roots," *South China Morning Post*, November 7, 2017.

30. Christoffer Bodeen, "China Widens Personality Cult Around 'Unrivaled Helmsman' Xi," *AP News*, November 22, 2017.

31. "習近平玩轉潮州｜大媽合十當神咁拜爆紅 網民鬧擾民即被警截圖" [Xi enjoys himself in Chaozhou—an elderly lady that worships him like a god becomes famous. Net citizens who cause disturbances are arrested by the police], *HK Golden*.

32. "习近平现身地铺金砖？专家：投习所好" [A gold brick where Xi Jinping trod? Expert: flattery for Xi], *Tang Dynasty Television*, January 2, 2021, www.ntdtv.com/gb/2021/01/02/a103022925.html.

33. "習近平南巡後潮汕鋪金磚搞崇拜 評論員：地方官投其所好望升官發財" [After Xi Jinping's southern tour gold bricks were set down in homage. Commentator: Local officials satisfy his every wish to obtain promotion and wealth], *Apple Daily*, February 2, 2021, .

34. Wang Yong, "Believers Forced to Worship China's Only God—President Xi," Association for the Defense of Human Rights and Religious Freedom, December 7, 2019, https://en.adhrrf.org/believers-forced-to-worship-chinas-only-god-president-xi.html.

35. Simon Denyer, "Jesus Won't Save You, Xi Jinping Will—Chinese Christians Told," *Washington Post*, November 14, 2017.

36. Gan, "Want to Escape Poverty?"; Tang Fen, "Xi Jinping's Quotes Replace the Ten Commandments in Churches," *Bitter Winter*, September 14, 2019.

37. Bodeen, "China Widens Personality Cult."

38. Márquez, "Two Models of Political Leader Cults," 278.

39. "Players 'Applaud' Xi Jinping in Tencent Game," *BBC News*.

40. Nathan Vanderklippe, "With a New App, China Claps Until Their Fingertips Ache for President Xi Jinping," *Globe and Mail*, October 19, 2017.

41. William Callahan quoted in Eleanor Peake, "China's New Viral App Could Be Straight out of Black Mirror," *Wired*, October 28, 2017.

42. Max Weber, "The Sociology of Charismatic Authority," in M. Weber, H. Gerth, and C. W. Mills (eds.), *From Max Weber: Essays in Sociology* (New York: Oxford University Press, 1946), 245, 294–295, and 299.

43. E. A. Rees, "Leader Cults: Varieties, Preconditions and Functions," in Balázs Apor et al. (eds.), *The Leader Cult in Communist Dictatorships* (London: Palgrave Macmillan, 2004), 20–21.

44. Glassman describes how it is usual that "the leadership clan" contributes to the process of producing a charismatic leader in "Legitimacy and Manufactured Charisma," 624.

45. Brown, *The World According to Xi*, 41.

46. See, for example, Zhang Shaoying and Derek McGhee, *China's Ethical Revolution and Regaining Legitimacy: Reforming the Communist Party Through Its Public Servants* (Cham, Switzerland: Palgrave Macmillan, 2017), 29.

47. Several researchers point to this effect of personality cults and charismatic leaders. See, for example, Rees, "Leader Cults," 11; Glassman, "Legitimacy and Manufactured Charisma," 630.

48. Glassman, "Legitimacy and Manufactured Charisma," 636.

49. See p. 6 in Wang Zheng, "The Chinese Dream: Concept and Context," *Journal of Chinese Political Science* 19 (2013): 1–13.

50. Zhang and McGhee, *China's Ethical Revolution*, 38.

51. Rees points out that one effect of the personality cult for participants is that their lives gain a deeper meaning and their longing for something beyond the worldly and banal is satisfied. See Rees, "Leader Cults," 12.

52. Emile Durkheim, *The Elementary Forms of the Religious Life* (London: George Allen & Unwin, 1915).

53. Glassman, "Legitimacy and Manufactured Charisma," 625.

54. Márquez, "Two Models of Political Leader Cults," 278.

55. For more about how the personality cult and charismatic leadership can create bigger goals for people's lives, see, for example, Rees, "Leader Cults," 11; Glassman, "Legitimacy and Manufactured Charisma," 630.

56. Leslie Nguyen-Okwu, "Hitler Had a Salute, Mao Had a Dance," *Ozy*, December 12, 2016, www.ozy.com/true-and-stories/hitler-had-a-salute-mao-had-a-dance/74076.

57. Quoted in Tom Mitchell, "The Chinese Control Revolution: The Maoist Echoes of Xi's Power Play," *Financial Times*, September 6, 2021.

58. Cheng Li argues for this in "Chairman Xi Crushes Dissent but Poor Believe He's Making China Great," *The Guardian*, October 14, 2017.

59. Quoted in Jacobs and Buckley, "Move Over Mao."

60. Tong Yanqi, "Morality, Benevolence, and Responsibility: Regime Legitimacy in China from Past to the Present," *Journal of Chinese Political Science* 16, no. 2 (2011): 141–159.

61. Tong, "Morality, Benevolence, and Responsibility," 151.

62. Daniel K. Gardner, quoted in Didi Kirsten Tatlow, "Confucian, Stubborn and Macho: China's Leader Is 'Xi Bigbig,'" *New York Times*, October 22, 2014.

63. Lucien Pye, *Asian Power and Politics: The Cultural Dimensions of Authority* (Cambridge, MA: Belknap Press of Harvard University Press, 1985), 66.

64. Glassman, "Legitimacy and Manufactured Charisma," 630.

65. Andrew J. Nathan, "The Puzzle of Authoritarian Legitimacy," *Journal of Democracy* 31, no. 1 (2020): 158–168.

66. Nathan, "The Puzzle of Authoritarian Legitimacy."

67. Tom Philips, "Chinese Protesters Use Steamed Buns to Voice Anger," *The Telegraph*, January 14, 2014.

68. TwtSignin (@TwtSignin), "提一个商业创意，开发梁家河牌包子的同时，要配套开发梁家河牌保鲜套，这样可以把梁家河牌包子卖到全世界，理论上卖到外星也可以，" Twitter, July 3, 2018, https://twitter.com/TwtSignin/status/1014113050578673664.

69. "習近平南巡後" [After Xi Jinping's southern tour], *Apple Daily*.

70. "Xi Jinping Game Show," BBC News.

71. Vanderklippe, "With a New App, China Claps."

72. Márquez, "Two Models of Political Leader Cults," 270.

73. Jean-Pierre Cabestan, "Political Changes in China since the 19th CCP Congress: Xi Jinping Is Not Weaker but More Contested," *East Asia* 36 (2019): 1–21, https://link.springer.com/article/10.1007/s12140-019-09305-x; Oki Nagai, "China Dials Down Xi's Personality Cult as Criticism Mounts," *Nikkei*, July 24, 2018.

74. "担心唤醒文革记忆 传各地机关禁挂习近平肖像" [Local authorities have been forbidden to hang up portraits of Xi Jinping out of fear of awakening memories of the Cultural Revolution], New Tang Dynasty Television, July 10, 2018, www.ntdtv.com/gb/2018/07/10/a1382836.html.

75. Nathan Vandeklippe, "'Big Daddy Xi' No More: Why China's President Has Been Tamped Down," *Globe and Mail*, May 7, 2016.

76. See Brian Hart, "Creating the Cult of Xi Jinping: The Chinese Dream as a Leader Symbol," *Cornell International Affairs Review* 9 (2016).

77. Márquez, "Two Models of Political Leader Cults," 278.

78. "習近平南巡後" [After Xi Jinping's southern tour], *Apple Daily*.

79. Glassman, "Legitimacy and Manufactured Charisma," 623.

80. Frank Dikötter quoted in Vanderklippe, "New App, China Claps."

# 5

# An Ideological Renaissance

WHAT DOES XI JINPING WANT? DURING A VISIT TO THE NATIONAL Museum in Beijing on November 29, 2012, a few days after he had been applauded into office at the eighteenth party conference, Xi proclaimed he had a dream of a "great renewal of the Chinese nation."[1] Along with the six other members of the freshly elected Standing Committee of the Politburo, he added luster to the exhibition *The Road to Renewal*. The exhibition was dedicated to China's history from the 1839–1842 Opium War, which led to foreign invasion, civil war, and unimaginable sufferings for the population—what the Chinese know as "the century of humiliation"—through the founding of the Communist Party in 1921, the People's Republic in 1949, and up until today. The museum is by the Tiananmen Square in China's political heart, a stone's throw away from the old imperial palace and the mausoleum where Mao Zedong's embalmed corpse rests. The museum is the most important official arena Xi could have chosen to present his dream. "The Chinese dream" (中国梦) was to become his motto.

Xi was a new leader who many China observers thought would be a reformer who would reduce the party state's control over the economy in favor of private enterprise. He might even permit a certain opening in politics. Nicholas Kristof, a *New York Times* journalist, prophesized that "Mao's corpse would be dragged out of Tiananmen . . . and Nobel Peace Prize winner Liu Xiaobo would be set free from prison."[2] Kristof was not the only one to get it wrong. A number of politicians, journalists, and analysts, both in and outside China, had great expectations of Xi, who had painfully experienced the worst sides of authoritarian rule during the Cultural Revolution and sent his own daughter to Harvard.

All these predictions were more wishful thinking than insight. Five years after Xi came to power, Liu was the first Nobel laureate to die in captivity since the Nazis ruled Germany, and ten years into Xi's rule, Mao's embalmed body still rests in the mausoleum (though some rumors in Beijing suggest it is a wax copy). No opening of the economy or politics has yet taken place. In other words, Xi has a quite different dream for China than Western observers hoped for.

"Xi's thoughts" have been written into the constitution both of the party and the nation. For those of us who are concerned with political developments in China, *Xi Jinping: The Government of China* gives valuable insights into these thoughts. This is a rich, authoritative four-volume collection of speeches, interviews, and photos along with a biography of the country's leader.[3] An army of bureaucrats edited the four volumes. With each book containing more than 500 pages, Xi's literary successor to *Mao's Little Red Book* is voluminous. But Mao is still the most read in Xi's China.

## Mao Bucks You Up

"A general trend under the heavens is that after division comes union, after union division" (天下大勢, 分久必合, 合必分). In the classic novel *The Three Kingdoms*, written in the fourteenth century, the idea of a dynastic cycle (周期律, 朝代循环) is formulated poetically. According to this theory, all Chinese dynasties go through the following stages: A new ruler unites China, establishes a new dynasty, and claims "the mandate of heaven" (天命). He is chosen by heaven to reign. China prospers, and its population grows. Then come corruption, natural disasters, overpopulation, and peasant uprisings. All this is taken as a sure sign that the emperor has lost the mandate of heaven. This can happen if he proves incompetent. There then follows a chaotic and violent period in which many warlords rule over a divided land. Finally, one of them triumphs over the others, and a new sovereign, who has the mandate of heaven, emerges. Back to the start and the merry-go-round swings round once more.

The theory that all dynasties in the course of a few generations go from conquest through a flowering stage to decline and fall was for thousands of years a source of concern to the Chinese. For the emperors this cycle seemed as natural and inevitable as the dance of the seasons. And for modern Chinese leaders, the theory is a reminder that they cannot take their power for granted. Mao, the founder of the People's Republic, was very concerned with dynastic cycles and thoroughly studied *Comprehensive Mirror in Aid of Governance* (资治通鉴), a book edited by historian Sima Guang in 1084. The book is a chronological account of China's history in 294 volumes, comprising 3 million characters, from 402 BCE to 960 CE. Mao boasted to the other Communist leaders that he had read the book no less than seventeen times.[4] The Song emperor asked Sima Guang to write the book to investigate the experiences of earlier emperors so that future rulers could learn from them, avoid their errors, and be better rulers.

This was also the reason Mao was so obsessed with the book. Mao's solution for avoiding the dynastic cycle was to establish a people's "democracy" in China—a rule by permanent revolution with Mao as its conductor. But the solution brought anarchy and untold suffering for the Chinese people. The People's Republic survived Mao, and now, many years later, Xi struggles with the same worries. China's Communist Party needs not only to escape the cycle that eats dynasties for breakfast but also to rewrite the political rule book that led American political scientist Francis Fukuyama, in the euphoria aroused by the end of the Cold War, to proclaim the end of history and the victory of capitalist modernism. History was over for authoritarian Communist parties, he felt.[5] With the exception of North Korea, the People's Republic of China is the world's longest-lived Communist state. All the others fell long ago. Xi's challenge is to prove these historical forces are wrong and that China's Communist Party shall rule for all eternity, bringing stability and happiness to the Chinese people.

Xi Jinping's solution to the dynastic cycle is to urge the party cadres to arm themselves ideologically for continual struggle. In a speech he gave during visits to several southern cities in December 2012, just after he became general secretary, Xi asked his audience why the Soviet Communist Party had collapsed. To no one's surprise, Xi already knew the answer. According to him, the Soviet Union collapsed not because of its ailing economy but because its ideals and convictions staggered. To quote Xi, "Historical nihilism rejected Soviet Union history, CPSU history, Lenin, and Stalin; it messed up the thinking. As a result, party branches perished; the party could not even control the military. Therefore, a big party like the CPSU was dissipated; a big socialist power like the Soviet Union collapsed. This is a vital historical lesson."[6]

Xi's solution to the serious problems the party state faced in governing the country at the start of the twenty-first century was then a mighty re-ideologization of China. To avoid the fate of the Soviet Communist Party, he urged the party cadres to be unshakeable in the faith. He set them to study the true teaching, that is Xi's, and tightened the requirements for party membership. For a long time, people had streamed to the party for pragmatic reasons, Xi felt. Now there should be room only for true believers.

The man who applied for party membership ten times before being accepted has made it very hard to get in. The process includes, among other things, recommendations, interviews, and tests, as well as meticulous studies of the previously mentioned app (学习强国), whose name can literally be translated as "Study to Strengthen the Country" or, as a play on words, "Study Xi to Strengthen the Country," a clear sign of Xi's dominant position in the party.[7] According to the party's own statistics, only 12 percent of applicants were accepted in 2019.[8]

Xi Jinping's heavier emphasis on ideology is a break from the policy established by Deng Xiaoping. Under and after Deng, Communist ideology was much weakened, and there was a widespread perception that the People's Republic was more Communist in name than in reality.

Then Xi plucked *Mao's Little Red Book* from his sleeve.

In the speech Xi held at the Party's Central School in January 2013, and as a continuation of the speech he had held a month earlier in connection with his trip to southern China, he argued that the three decades under Mao and the thirty years of reform under Deng were equally important and valuable. According to Xi, "The period of history after Reform and Opening Up cannot be used to negate the period of history before Opening Up and Reform; and the period of history before Opening Up and Reform cannot be used to negate the period of history after Reform and Opening Up." This position became known as "irrefutables" (两个不能否定), meaning that one cannot reject Mao's policies because of Deng, and vice versa.[9] In other words, the course set in 1949 must on the whole be followed. Xi's predecessors had also referred to Mao, the founder of the People's Republic, but then more out of a sense of duty and with a sense of shame. Xi, on the other hand, embraced Mao with both arms. While his predecessors said that Mao's policies were "30 percent wrong, 70 percent right," under Xi the percentage has been adjusted in the old chairman's favor. In a speech held on the occasion of Mao's 120th birthday, Xi broke with party orthodoxy requiring him to mention the former leader's mistakes. Instead the speech was almost a hymn of praise.[10]

Long before Xi came to power, the leadership in Beijing was well aware that the system was sick. The symptoms were corruption, growing dissatisfaction, and weakened economic growth. But how did Xi get from diagnosis to treatment? Why did he think ideological decline was the cause of the disease? Why on earth did he embrace Mao, the tyrant who sent the young Xi to forced reschooling and persecuted his family and brought disaster to millions of Chinese of his generation?

A plausible explanation is that Xi has an instrumental relationship with Mao; that is, he sees revitalizing the old chairman as an effective way of revitalizing the party and "making China great again." Mao is after all the man who reestablished order under heaven by defeating foreign occupiers, nationalists, and numerous warlords, ending a century of humiliation by founding the People's Republic. The regime can claim that it stands on the shoulders of "five thousand years of uninterrupted civilization," but it is still young and absolutely cannot take its power for granted. The Communist Party has only ruled for seventy years. Xi and his cronies must then establish their own origin myth. Mao is unavoidable. Criticizing Mao is criticizing the whole system; weakening him is weakening the whole system.[11]

But this is not the entire explanation. We certainly cannot claim we can look inside Xi's head, but it may seem that Xi's embrace of Mao comes not just from the brain but also from the heart. As French China observer François Bougon points out, it is a myth that the Chinese put away *Mao's Little Red Book* after his death. The ideology is alive and kicking, particularly among Xi's generation, who were brought up listening to stories of the heroes who took part in the Long March and fought for a Communist China. The cult of the red heroes is just as strong as that of the saints in the Catholic Church.[12] As Xi is the son of one of Mao's closest war companions, Xi Zhongxun, his historic universe is full of the red heroes. Xi probably has a deep admiration for Mao, both the former leader's policies and his style.

Besides there is little to indicate that Xi blames Mao personally for what happened to him and his family. Jean Philippe Béja, professor at Science-Po in Paris, thinks the generation that experienced this ordeal went one of two ways. One group turned against the Communist Party. Liu Xiaobo is an example of this. The other developed a nostalgic relationship to the period and a strong feeling of belonging to the party. The Cultural Revolution is a complicated period with contrasting and opposing narratives. On the one hand, we have the previously mentioned "scar literature," and on the other we have the versions of what we might call the "revolutionary romantics." Some would claim that their years in the countryside were the best of their lives, characterized by a relatively uncomplicated youth free from parental control, with strong bonds to other city youngsters sent to do forced labor there, with whom they made friends for life and even fell in love. Xi definitely belongs with those who strengthened their ties to the party during and after these turbulent years.[13]

## To the Left

In accordance with the concept of "irrefutables," during his first decade in office, Xi sought to maneuver so that the heritages of Mao and Deng were reasonably equally treated. Under the latter, ideology became more peripheral. Economic development was the main goal, almost regardless of the policy needed to achieve it. Deng Xiaoping set this new course in 1982, calling it "socialism with Chinese characteristics." The private sector, foreign capital, and other capitalist phenomena were no longer strictly forbidden abominations but permitted and even desired. The economy changed direction, moving toward a market economy though still imprinted with the party's plans. This trend reached a high point when China became a member of the World Trade Organization in 2001. Under Jiang Zemin and Hu Jintao, China seemed, both to the world and to its citizens, like a capitalist country in all but name. You had to look long and hard to discover any sign of Marxist-Leninist ideology in Chinese society. Economic growth was the top priority. And the growth was formidable, unique in the history of humanity. More than half a billion Chinese were raised out of poverty between 1981 and 2004, according to the World Bank.[14]

When Xi Jinping laid a wreath before a bronze statue of former leader Deng Xiaoping in Shenzhen during a visit to southern China in December 2012, the message was obvious for most China observers. It was Deng's famous "southern journey" at the end of the 1970s that was the starting shot for his economic reforms and China's extraordinary growth. Was this not a sign that Xi intended to continue along this path? After all, his late father, Xi Zhongxun, had been handpicked by Deng to govern the unruly Guangdong Province and to be in charge of the establishment of Shenzhen as a so-called special economic zone—that is, an area granted greater freedom than the rest of China to pursue a more investment-friendly policy.

Xi has continued to use southern China as a test area for economic opening to the world, and he has especially invested in the Greater Bay Area (GBA). This lies at the estuary of the Pearl River, has a population of 71.2 million, and includes nine megacities in Guangdong Province—Guangzhou, Shenzhen, Zhuhai, Foshan, Dongguan, Zhongshan, Jiangmen, Huizhou, and Zhaoqing—as well as the two special administrative regions, Hong Kong and Macau. At the time of writing, these cities and the regions together constitute the world's twelfth-largest economy, bigger than Russia's.[15] Here we can find China's most innovative technology companies, Huawei,

ZTE, DJI, and Tencent (the parent company of WeChat), and start-up companies abound. For these reasons many expect that GBA will be Asia's answer to Silicon Valley. Beijing's ambition is for GBA to play a leading role as a center of innovation for the global economy by 2035, with a total economy greater than that of both the United Kingdom and France.[16]

But at the same time as he has continued Deng's policy, Xi has, in key areas, turned the party and the country leftward.[17] When Xi came to power, two different directions dominated within the party, with two aspiring leaders: Wang Yang, who was party secretary in Guangzhou, stood for market reform; Bo Xilai, who was party secretary in Chongqing and the son of another founder of the People's Republic, believed that the party should instead revitalize the basic revolutionary values that once brought it to power. The latter's policy is clearly illustrated by the neo-Maoist campaign that became his signature slogan: "Sing red and strike black" (唱紅打黑). "Red" means go to the left, which in the Chinese political context means to oppose reform and strengthen state control over the economy, and "black" means to combat crime and corruption.[18] Xi chose Wang as a member of the Politburo's Standing Committee and contributed to Bo's fall. But he picked Bo's policy.

Xi had not long sat in the general secretary's chair before he, like Bo, had reintroduced Maoist methods into the party. In 2013 he introduced "mass line campaigns" to improve cadres' work style and bring the party closer to the people. Party members should learn to live sparingly, avoid waste, and lead simple lives. Members were to endure criticism and self-criticism until they "blushed and sweated" in good old-fashioned Mao-era style. Xi believed that the "self-criticism's knife" had become too blunt and rusty.[19] Xi gave this speech when he had just come to power, and it is easy to read this as a concealed criticism of the lack of ideological discipline under his predecessors. Party members shall not only have the correct political orientation but also "recognise virtues, follow social ethics, control personal lust, observe moral standards, maintain integrity and cultivate character," and "resist the temptations of power, money and sex."[20]

In Xi's China, party schools are up-and-coming. All over the country, the latest ideological messages are communicated to packed classes. Recently, the party has a particular focus on educating its members about Xi Jinping's teachings. More and more research centers are being opened to study the leader's ideas in depth. The first ten were started in 2017, the same year Xi's thoughts were officially incorporated into the constitution. Afterward more followed, putting the spotlight on such themes as the military, diplomacy, economy, law and order, and "ecological education." This extensive thematic range emphasizes that Xi thinks big thoughts about most things. Most of these centers are linked to major places of learning such as Peking University, Tsinghua University, the Chinese Academy for the Social Sciences, and the Central Party School. According to the news bureau *Xinhua*, eighteen such research centers existed by the summer of 2021.[21]

Moreover, Xi puts much greater weight than his predecessors on the spiritual and emotional bond between the population and the party. "If an official does not act on behalf of the people, it is better for him to go home and sell sweet potatoes," emphasizes Xi.[22] Work on ideology and thinking, words that recall Mao's ideological campaigns, is once more defined as vital for the party.[23] The party leadership experienced a collective moral crisis among the Chinese caused by the one-sided focus on individual economic happiness. In response, at the eighteenth party congress, the outgoing general secretary, Hu Jintao, presented twelve "socialist core values" (社会主义核心价值观). The twelve values, written in twenty-four Chinese characters, are the national values of prosperity, democracy, politeness, and harmony; the social values of liberty, equality, justice, and the rule of law; and the individual values of patriotism, dedication, integrity, and friendship.[24] Immediately Xi began to hammer these values into the heads of his citizens. He started patriotic campaigns to get the people to feel devotion to the party and engagement with and obligation to the party's historical goals and mission for China.

Xi Jinping has particularly emphasized the importance of building support for the party through the patriotic or political education of children and the young. In this way the youngest citizens of the People's Republic are indoctrinated in the right socialist values.[25] After Xi's thoughts were incorporated into the party constitution in 2017, his thoughts were introduced as topics for several of the country's universities and eagerly studied by the party's Youth League. In August 2021, the Education Department issued a directive obliging all educational institutions to promote Xi's ideas in the classroom (i.e., "Xilosophy" as curriculum). "To cultivate socialism's builders and successors with an all-round moral, intellectual, physical, and aesthetic grounding and an industrious spirit we must arm our students' minds with Xi's ideas about socialism with Chinese characteristics," as the directive puts it. Xi's thoughts pop up in the curriculum as naturally as grammar and mathematics. Brand new textbooks awaited expectant children and youth across China as they showed up for the first day of school on September 1, 2021. The books are full of quotes from Xi and pictures of his smiling face. Primary school pupils read about the achievements of Chinese civilization, the role of the Communist Party in combatting poverty, and the successful handling of the Covid-19 pandemic. Xi's quotations about patriotism and citizens' duties are interspersed with anecdotes about his meetings with the man in the street. "Grandpa Xi Jinping is very busy with his job, but no matter how busy he is, he joins our activities and cares about our growth," a textbook says. Textbooks for older children go into more depth and ask more complicated questions, for example, about China's path to becoming a "modern socialist great power."[26]

Despite Xi's signals during the visit to Shenzhen, mentioned earlier, about continuing reform and opening, in the economic sphere too Xi has swung to the left—from market to planned economy. Among other things, Xi has reversed reforms Jiang Zemin introduced to reduce the state's role in state-owned enterprises (SOEs).[27] Xi has made clear that the party committees in these companies must approve all major decisions made by the companies, including employment of managers and key personnel to ensure that they are "politically qualified."[28] Another function of these company party committees is to arrange political lectures and other forms of political education of employees.[29] SOEs constitute "the material and political foundations of socialism with Chinese characteristics" and should be strengthened to become "the party's most reliable force," according to Xi.[30]

Xi has taken steps to promote the big SOEs at the expense of small and medium-sized firms. In Chinese this phenomenon is known as "state-owned advances, privately owned retreats" (国进民退). Opportunities for privatization and exposure to competition have been limited.[31] In contrast to small and medium-sized firms, SOEs enjoy various support schemes, such as easy access to favorable loans from state banks, cheap electricity, and special state tender schemes. During the Covid pandemic, for instance, few of the 20,000 companies awarded contracts to produce medical equipment and machines were private.[32] In Beijing officially, both private and state companies are needed; in reality, private companies are being incorporated into the state economy. In Hong Kong some say sarcastically that Xi seems to think private firms have accomplished their historic mission, so the party can go back to state-owned enterprises.[33]

Xi has also strangled Chinese civil society. Until he took power there was a vital civil society invigorated by the spontaneous response to the Sichuan earthquake disaster of 2008. Now there is little room for such engagement. Under Xi China has become steadily more authoritarian, some say even totalitarian. Michael Clarke, a China researcher at Australian National University and an expert on the Uighurs in Xinjiang, thinks that Xi has ambitions to control not only the bodies but also the minds of the Chinese, thus taking China in a more totalitarian direction.[34] Xi has tasked the party with nothing less than managing people's thinking: "To better guide people in their ways of thinking and strengthening their theoretical education is a top task for internal Party political activities and a prerequisite to ensuring concerted action."[35]

In this political climate, the space for alternative, divergent thoughts has become highly restricted. Everyone who can be conceived as a threat to Xi—political dissidents, social activists, ideological liberals, and others—must be silenced. Religious communities are especially exposed. Christians are persecuted and churches closed. The situation is the same for religious minorities such as Tibetan Buddhists and Muslims. Allegedly, more than a million Uighurs have been forcibly interned in what the Chinese authorities call "reeducation camps" in Xinjiang Province, where, according to the party paper the *Global Times*, they are retrained to become "normal people" (i.e., Han).[36] Many have pointed out that, more than anything else, the camps resemble concentration camps, and according to human rights organizations and Western authorities, Beijing's treatment of the Uighurs can be regarded as a cultural genocide since reeducation involves eliminating Uighurs' culture, not just their religion but their language and other sources of identity.[37] In September 2022, the outgoing UN human rights head, Michelle Bachelet, despite pressure from Beijing, published a report on Xinjiang, confirming that the treatment of the Uighur ethnic group "may include crimes against humanity."[38]

Xi is ever turning against new groups—the most recent being the country's wealthy elite, especially those linked with the technology sector and entertainment. In October 2020 Jack Ma, China's richest man and the founder of Alibaba, the country's biggest and one of the world's most valuable internet companies, fell out of favor with Xi. This caused several China observers to predict that shareholders and investors would flee the tech industry. But this is a price Xi is willing to pay to strengthen his grip on the sector. Next, several of China's biggest celebrities, such as actors Zhao Wei and Zheng Shuang and the blogger Feng Xiaoyi, fell victim to Xi's wrath. According to the authorities these celebrities were far from possessing the values advocated by the party. The latter was accused of being 娘炮, a derogatory term for men regarded as feminine. In Xi's China there is no room for feminine men, and films regarded as promoting homosexuality are censored. The authorities also target fan clubs and force talent competitions and reality shows off the air, arguing they promote false values. In this way Xi tightens his grip on private business and pop culture. In Xi's China only one celebrity can be cultivated: Xi.

Norwegian Oxford professor Stein Ringen describes Xi's China as a "controlocracy."[39] In using new technology to control the population, the country's authoritarian authorities have created something that recalls an Orwellian dictatorship. What primarily affects most Chinese is that this technology is linked to the social credit system. This system ranks the reliability of individuals, firms, and public institutions. Rewards and punishments are dished out according to the ranking.

The system is tightly linked to mass surveillance and facial-recognition programs. An estimated 600 million surveillance cameras keep tabs on the Chinese. Rated by the number of cameras per 1,000 inhabitants, eight of the ten most monitored cities in the world are in China. In the megacity Chongqing there is no danger of being overlooked as there are 163 cameras per 1,000 inhabitants.[40] In Shenzhen, neighbor to Hong Kong, red lights not only register those who cross with the aid of facial-recognition technology, but their photos are posted on large screens nearby with their previous red-light offences listed—to public scorn.[41]

WeChat (微信, *Weixin*) is an app most Chinese have. Now it has so many functions, it is hard to do without. It is Facebook, PayPal, eBay, Kombo, Uber Eats, Skype, and much more, all in one. Because technology companies are obliged by law to share consumer data with the authorities, the latter have access to all the information that passes through the unencrypted app, potentially gathering colossal amounts of information about large parts of the Chinese population.

In June 2013 a classified party document, "Communiqué on the Present Situation in the Ideological Sphere," was leaked. Known as Document 9, as it was the central committee's nineth document that year, it gave detailed insight into Xi's program. The document instructed the party to oppose what it called "false ideological trends, opinions and activities," no matter where they occurred, and "absolutely under no circumstances to permit any chance of, or platform for, wrong thinking or opinions to spread." It listed seven ideological errors to avoid:[42]

1. Promoting Western constitutional democracy
2. Promoting universal values in an attempt to weaken the theoretical foundation of the party's leadership
3. Promoting civil society in an attempt to weaken the governing party's social base
4. Promoting neoliberalism or trying to change China's economic system
5. Promoting the Western idea of journalism, challenge China's principle that the media and publishing shall be subordinated to party discipline
6. Promoting historical nihilism or trying to undermine the history of the Chinese Communist Party and the New China
7. Questioning "reform and opening" and the socialist nature of socialism with Chinese characteristics

This shows that Xi believes he is fighting an intense and complex war against "anti-Chinese forces" attempting to undermine the People's Republic with "Western" ideas of universalism, democracy, freedom of expression, and other individual human rights. Xi believes that if one capitulates to such values, these forces will destroy both China's unique development model and the stability the Chinese benefit from and which depends on the Communist Party's monopoly of power. Accordingly, the country must combat what Document 9 refers to as false ideological trends and stand up for its own system. The key to success in this war is "fourfold self-confidence" (四个自信). This has become a key slogan under Xi. It urges party members, officials, and the Chinese people to be "confident in our chosen way, confident in our leading theories, confident in our political system, and confident in our culture." While the first three were part of the party rhetoric before Xi took over, he added the last point. This emphasizes how he tries to combine communism with traditional Chinese culture and history.[43]

That is why it is vital for Xi to own the narrative of China's history. In the list of the seven false ideological trends, we find historical nihilism, which in this context is questioning the party's official view of China's history. In Xi's China, only *one* view of history is allowed: that the party rescued China from poverty, chaos, and dissolution and made it a great power again. In this story there are many heroes, but the greatest of them all are Mao and Xi.

## Back to the Future

For Xi, the Communist Party—under his leadership—is the only guarantee of a strong and united China, a China that will never again be a victim, that will proudly take its place in the world on its own terms.[44] A proverb says, "He who controls the past controls the present and the future," which is why Xi is so concerned with the role the Communist Party plays in modern Chinese history. When the party with Mao at its head came to power in 1949, the country was in ruins. The party presents itself as ending the century of humiliation that began with the First Opium War and European intervention. The party was the driving force behind China's throwing off its foreign shackles, reuniting, and rising as a great power.

One month after Xi held his famous speech in the National Museum in Beijing, on November 29, 2012, he elaborated on what he meant by his Chinese dream:

> Everyone has an ideal, ambition and dream. We are now talking about the Chinese Dream. In my opinion, achieving the rejuvenation of the Chinese nation has been the greatest dream of the Chinese people since the advent of modern times. This dream embodies the long-cherished hope of several generations of Chinese people, gives expression to the overall interests of the Chinese nation and the Chinese people, and represents the shared aspiration of all the sons and daughters of the Chinese nation. . . . I firmly believe that the goal of bringing about a moderately prosperous society in all respects can be achieved by 2021, when CPC [Chinese Communist Party] celebrates its centenary; the goal of building China into a modern socialist country that is prosperous, strong, democratic, culturally advanced, and harmonious can be achieved by 2049, when the People's Republic of China marks its centenary; and the dream of the rejuvenation of the Chinese nation will then be realized.[45]

The goals Xi refer to have become known as the "two centenary goals" (两个一百年). They are intended to lay the foundations for the realization of his dreams for a future China. However, the two centenary goals are not new; Jiang Zemin and Hu Jintao had introduced them earlier. Xi simply reaffirmed them. Xi, though, has an exceptional ability to raise up certain ideas, give them new life, and make them his own political slogans.

In 2021, the year the Chinese Communist Party celebrated its centenary, Xi acclaimed the fulfilment of the first of the two centenary goals, which was that China had become "a moderately prosperous country." The term *moderately prosperous* (小康) has its roots in both Confucianism and Chinese Communist theory. In old Chinese thinking this indicates a society whose inhabitants can live comfortable but ordinary lives. Deng Xiaoping was the first in more recent times to use the term as a goal for the economic reforms he launched at the end of the 1970s. But for most Chinese the concept is fairly abstract. To make it easier to grasp, the party chose to say it was a success if the gross national product had doubled from 2010 to 2021. In a country where the authorities change the terrain to suit the map, it was not so surprising that the statisticians calculated that the target had been reached.

So Xi was on schedule to achieve the Chinese dream of a prosperous great power. In 2049, the centennial of the People's Republic, the second goal is according to the plan to be reached. Then China will be "a strong, democratic, civilized, harmonious and modern socialist society." Xi reads the history of the People's Republic as a drama in three acts:

Act 1: Mao directs China's recovery.
Act 2: Deng ensures China becomes prosperous.
Act 3: Xi directs China becoming great.

Finally, China has entered "the new era."

The key historic role of Xi was affirmed through a resolution at the plenum meeting of the Central Committee of the party in late autumn 2021. This was the third resolution the party had ever passed about history and such an important event that China observers followed it with Argus eyes. The first, passed in 1945, approved by Mao Zedong, gave the official version of the first twenty-four years of the Chinese Communist Party's struggle to survive the nationalists and Japanese occupants. The wording affirmed Mao as undisputed leader of the party. Thirty-six years later, in 1981, the second history resolution was passed with Deng's blessing. A compromise resolved the inflamed issue of Mao's heritage. Ideological concepts such as the class struggle and a state-controlled planned economy were chucked into history's dustbin, and this opened the way for Deng's pragmatic policies and reforms.

The third resolution is different from the first two in that it is not much about the past and far more about power and visions for shaping China's future. Or, to put it another way, it legitimizes Xi as ruler indefinitely. The two-hundred-page *A Short History of the Communist Party* restructures the official party history so that it naturally culminates in the perfect leadership of Xi Jinping. The resolution affirms that Xi is a man of unique intellect and leadership abilities. Among other things, one can read that the Central Committee, with

Xi at its top, has "shown great historic initiative, incredible political courage and a powerful ability to set goals." It goes on to establish Xi's "thoughts about socialism with Chinese characteristics for a new era" as governing the party's future and, not least, securing his position as the core of the Central Committee as well as the party. In other words, the resolution affirms Xi's historic role as the one who will make China great again.[46]

Although the centenary goals are vaguely formulated, it is important not to underestimate the substance of Xi Jinping's Chinese dream. It shares many of the materialistic components of the American dream. Chinese society shall become prosperous, and its citizens shall be able to travel, study, and realize themselves. But at the same time—and even more importantly—the Chinese dream focuses on "the renewal of the nation" to a position of prosperity and might.[47] While the American dream is individualist, the Chinese version puts far more weight on the nation. Xi's concept of "renewal" is synonymous with "restoration," that is improving what once was and making it new again. That makes it interesting to ask what Xi and the party want to bring back and make new again. Which epoch of China's 5,000-year uninterrupted civilization does he intend to bring back to take the nation into the future?

According to Victor K. Fong, China researcher at the Australian National University, the Tang Dynasty in particular seems the ideal for Xi's dream.[48] Memories of this dynasty (618–907), reckoned the gold age of Chinese civilization, are cultivated to this day. In Chinese official discourse it is presented as the ideal—a wealthy, educated, and cosmopolitan empire. Art, culture, and innovation flourished. In its time the Tang empire was the biggest and strongest in the world, with an estimated population of 50 million, and the capital Chang'an (today's Xi'an) was the biggest city in the world with 1 million inhabitants. What is known within Chinese philosophy as "the three schools" (三教), Confucianism, Taoism, and Buddhism, lived side by side. China had a good government by the standards of the time, and Chinese culture spread to large parts of Asia.

The Middle Kingdom was a magnet for people from faraway shores, who flocked to the country to admire its wonders. The Silk Road, which passed through central and southern Asia, the Middle

East, Iran, and Turkey, all the way to Rome, was at its busiest. Envoys from other countries came to pay their respects to the mighty Tang emperor, and foreign merchants brought exotic goods from distant lands. Students came from Korea, India, and elsewhere to study poetry, literature, music, dance, calligraphy, and painting and in search of new wisdom to bring back to their own peoples. China had diplomatic relations with seventy countries, and more than 10,000 foreigners lived in their own quarters in the capital. The Middle Kingdom enjoyed recognition and respect.

For Xi the nation's great renewal is a restoration of China in the spirit of the magnificent Tang Dynasty. Nationalism has been an integral part of the Communist Party since its inception in 1921 and was particularly strong under Mao.[49] But a civilization-based nationalism has gained a far more dominant position under Xi. His dream is about China enjoying recognition and respect. Under the Tang Dynasty, Chinese civilization and culture reached out to the rest of the world along the Silk Road. Xi plans to do the same with his Belt and Road scheme. "One belt, one road" (一带一路) is a massive plan for the development of infrastructure and the economy initiated by Xi. The word *belt* designates plans to build a network of trading routes across the entire Eurasian continent in the form of high-speed trains, motorways, and ports to link Asia, the Middle East, and Europe once more with China.[50] In Xi's vision the Communist Party is the embodiment of Chinese civilization, and criticizing the party is therefore the same as criticizing the Chinese nation.

Earlier the party accepted the country's ethnic minorities. Mao believed that all of China's officially recognized ethnic minorities should be allowed to keep their own identities, and any suspicion of Han chauvinism was vigorously suppressed. The Han Chinese (汉族) are the country's largest ethnic group, making up about 90 percent of the total population. In agreement with established practice, Xi has repeatedly warned against the dangers of Han chauvinism on the one side and local ethnic nationalism on the other.[51] Nonetheless, in the bigger picture, Han chauvinism has been freer to act. After all, Xi has spoken of Han culture as "the nation's soul," as acceptance of the minorities has diminished.[52] Han identity has become a goal for all Chinese citizens; minorities such as Uighurs, Tibetans, Mongols, and others are expected to renounce their own culture and language and become like the majority. This is in line with the general demand to conform to whatever the party requires—what language to use, what to think, how to behave.

Han-centered Chinese nationalism has been on the march since the 1990s. This is expressed through the Hanfu movement, which has a huge following among Chinese youngsters. The movement is important as it is one of the clearest expressions of Han nationalism in Xi's China. Hanfu (汉 服) means "Han dress." Central to this movement is dressing in the traditional clothes worn by the Han majority for much of the land's history, with the exception of the Qing Dynasty, which made Manchu dress compulsory.

Several online celebrities have embraced the fashion, which has helped spread the trend. Among these is Li Ziqi, one of China's best-known food, country life, and social media influencers. She sews her own Han-inspired clothes and promotes a traditional rural lifestyle in picturesque landscapes. In January 2021 she set a world record for a Chinese-language YouTube channel with her more than 14 million followers.[53]

Since he came to power in 2012, Xi Jinping has actively promoted a Han-centered idea of the Chinese cultural heritage to strengthen patriotism and national identity. Beijing's support for this cultural awakening has indubitably given Hanfu society energy.[54] Since 2018 the Communist Party's Youth League has arranged an annual Hanfu Day to celebrated traditional costumes as an important cultural expression.[55]

## Up with Han Feizi

Xi Jinping embraces China's cultural heritage. Visits to museums and places of significance for Chinese culture and history are nearly always on the agenda when he visits the provinces. Xi frequently mentions Chinese words of wisdom—proverbs of Confucius, Sun Tzu, Mencius, Laozi, Han Feizi, and others who have contributed to China's intellectual history. In a speech he gave at Peking University in 2014, he pronounced that Chinese culture is "a part of people's

DNA, anchored in people's hearts" and something that imperceptibly affects the way the Chinese think and act. He quoted various Chinese philosophers no less than forty times.[56]

In other words, Xi loves the classics. Undoubtedly, Confucius is the one he most frequently quotes in his speeches, but if one examines Xi's politics, then, according to Chinese American author Zha Jianying, there is good reason to think he is more influenced by another Chinese philosopher: Han Feizi.[57] Han Feizi (280–233 BCE) belonged to the philosophical school known as *legalism.* This school emphasized that rulers had to rule their subjects through laws that applied to all and punish harshly anyone who broke them. Legalism became the state philosophy under the Qin Dynasty (221–207 BCE), a short-lived, authoritarian regime that united most of the Chinese kingdoms under an iron-fisted terror regime. Later Confucianism became the dominant philosophical direction. While Confucius believed that humans are basically good, especially if they have a good model in the emperor, Han Feizi's philosophy is founded on the idea that humanity is evil and selfish and therefore must be ruled through strict laws and harsh punishments. Han Feizi thinks a ruler can trust in no one near him, not even his wife or children, because they are bound to him not by devotion but rather by self-interest. To keep his subjects under control, Han Feizi asserts that the ruler must acquire a big toolbox containing a wide range of practical strategies and psychological tricks. No one should know what he is up to. He should be sly, cunning, and secretive. He should use fear, secrecy, lies, surveillance, spies, divide-and-rule tactics, blackmail, and loyalty tests. Qin Hui, historian and professor at Tsinghua University, claims that Chinese leaders have always been Confucians on the outside but legalists at heart and therefore ruled through fear and control.[58]

Xi has rehabilitated Han Feizi, often quoting the old philosopher's thoughts in his speeches. Xi also practices the latter's principles for good governance. In 2014, using Han Feizi's power recipe, Xi announced "the four-pronged comprehensive strategy" (四个全面战略布局), a list of goals for China. These are to build a moderately prosperous society, to expand in-depth reform, to promote law-based governance, and to enforce strict party governance.[59] The goals built on Deng Xiaoping's thoughts but put far greater weight on the rule of law.[60] During the seventy years the People's Republic has existed so far, the party by and large has maintained a de jure distinction between it and the state, including the legal system, despite the party's de facto controlling the state apparatus and frequently disregarding the law. Xi wiped out this distinction by letting the party take over all the state domains, including legislative powers.[61]

In Xi's first decade in power, 70 percent of all existing party rules have been revised or added, as a check on the home page of the party's Organization Department proves.[62] None of his predecessors were anywhere near so active in changing the rules or adding new ones.[63] And no one need doubt his readiness to mercilessly persecute and punish rule breakers, be they flies or tigers.

Whether consciously or not, Xi follows Han Feizi's exhortations to rulers to let no one know what they are up to. To his subjects the ruler should be a blank: they should know nothing about what he wants or what he is thinking so that no one can curry favor or influence him. This is an art Xi has honed to perfection.[64]

## Conclusion

Is there a Xi-ism as there is a Maoism? Xi Jinping's thoughts about "socialism with Chinese characteristics for a new era" are now part of both the constitution of the party and the state, a great honor for him. Despite this recognition, it hard to find a single ideological concept that Xi has produced by himself. Even if Xi is the first Chinese Communist leader to use the word *dream* about his vision for China, there is nothing new about leaders having dreams for their countries. Mao dreamed of China as a Communist ideal society and, during the Cultural Revolution, of China as the center of a global revolution. Deng dreamed about the "modernization of China," Jiang of "the great renewal of the Chinese nation," and Hu of "a harmonious society."

Central ideas such as "the two centenary goals," "the four-pronged comprehensive strategy," and "the twelve core socialist values" are also continuations of ideas introduced by Xi's predecessors. One might also claim that the "new silk road," another of Xi's signature programs, continues political initiatives to motivate Chinese companies to invest overseas dating back to the 1990s.

Oppression, anticorruption, and emphasis on big state corporations were hardly things Xi initiated; in reality, they were old policies. Early signs of tightening political control and oppression came after Charter 8, a political manifesto for reform signed by 303 Chinese officials, lawyers, and intellectuals and published on Human Rights Day in 2008. China's more assertive foreign policy, which we shall examine in the next chapter, began after the 2008 Beijing Olympics, which boosted the country's confidence—four years before Xi entered the world stage.

So, to a large extent, Xi has carried on the ideological lines of his predecessors. This reflects a system that emphasizes continuity in long, strategic, political lines. However, that said, we must acknowledge Xi's undoubted ability to dust off old hits and compose an interesting playlist. Xi raises up old ideological concepts, gives them his own distinctive twist, and puts them together to make strong ideological foundations for the party and himself. In this way he hopes to avoid the "dynastic cycle," a curse that has menaced every Chinese ruler, and ensure that the party becomes the force that restores the Chinese people's lost honor and brings prosperity and power.

## Notes

1. "Xi Highlights National Goal of Rejuvenation," *Xinhua*, November 30, 2012, www.chinadaily.com.cn/china/2012-11/30/content_15972687.htm.
2. Kristof, "Looking for a Jump-Start."
3. Xi Jinping, *The Governance of China*. 4 vols. (Beijing: Foreign Language Press, 2014, 2017, 2020, and 2022).
4. Wang Yuhua, "Can the Chinese Communist Party Learn from Chinese Emperors?," in Jennifer Rudolf and Michael Szonyi (eds.), *The China Questions: Critical Insights into a Rising Power* (Cambridge, MA: Harvard University Press, 2018), 58.
5. Francis Fukuyama, *The End of History and the Last Man* (New York: The Free Press, 1992).
6. Li Zhuoran, "The CCP's Changing Understanding of the Soviet Union's Collapse," The Diplomat, October 8, 2022, https://thediplomat.com /2022/10/the-ccps-changing-understanding-of-the-soviet-unions-collapse/.

7. Neil Thomas, "Members Only: Recruitment Trends in the Chinese Communist Party Members," MacroPolo, July 15, 2015.

8. "Number of Submitted and Accepted Applications for the Chinese Communist Party (CCP) Membership in China from 2013 to 2021," Statista, July 27, 2021.

9. "习近平'两个不能否定'是实现'中国梦'的科学论断" [Xi Jinping's "the two irrefutables" is the scientific thesis for realizing the Chinese dream], *Zhongguo gongchandang xinwenwang*, May 10, 2013, http://cpc.people.com.cn/n/2013/0510/c241220-21441140.html.

10. Bougon, *Inside the Mind of Xi Jinping*, 89–91.

11. Bougon, *Inside the Mind of Xi Jinping*, 91.

12. Bougon, *Inside the Mind of Xi Jinping*, 95.

13. Conversation with Professor Jean-Philippe Beja, Sciences Po, Paris, June 11, 2019,

14. "China—From Poor Areas to Poor People: China's Evolving Poverty Reduction Agenda—an Assessment of Poverty and Inequality," World Bank, March 5, 2009, http://documents.worldbank.org/curated/en/816851468219918783/pdf/473490SR0CN0P010Disclosed0041061091.pdf.

15. "Statistics of the Guangdong–Hong Kong–Macao Greater Bay Area," Hong Kong Trade Development Council Research, June 18, 2019, http://hong-kong-economy-research.hktdc.com/business-news/article/Guangdong-Hong-Kong-Macau-Bay-Area/Statistics-of-the-Guangdong-Hong-Kong-Macao-Greater-Bay-Area/bayarea/en/1/1X000000/1X0AE3Q1.htm.

16. Lau Kelvin and Ding Shuang, "In GDP Race, the Greater Bay Area Could Overtake UK and France by 2035," *China Daily*, August 5, 2019.

17. Beach, "Leaked Speech."

18. Jason Y. Wu, "Categorical Confusion: Ideological Labels in China," Indiana University, September 9, 2020, https://papers.ssrn.com/sol3/papers.cfm?abstract_id=3699710.

19. "党的群众路线教育实践活动工作会议召开 习近平发表重要讲话" [The party has held a working conference on the program for mass line education and practice. Xi Jinping held an important speech], *Xinhua*, June 18, 2013, www.xinhuanet.com//politics/2013-06/18/c_116194026.htm; Xi Jinping, "The Guiding Thoughts and Goals for the Program of Mass Line Education and Practice," in *The Governance of China* (Beijing: Foreign Language Press, 2014), 1:410–416; Blanchette, *China's New Red Guards*, 139.

20. Xi Jinping, "Tighten Political Activities Within Our Party," in *The Governance of China* (Beijing: Foreign Language Press, 2017), 2:198; Xi Jinping, "Be a Good County Party Secretary," in *The Governance of China* (Beijing: Foreign Language Press, 2017), 2: 154.

21. "7 More Research Centers Established to Study Xi Jinping Thought," *Xinhua*, June 26, 2021, www.xinhuanet.com/english/2021-06/26/c_1310029353.htm.

22. Xi, "Be a Good County Party Secretary," 157.

23. "习近平强调'意识形态工作极端重要'有何深意" [What does Xi Jinping's emphasis on "ideological work is extremely important" mean?], *Zhongguo gongchandang xinwenwang*, August 21, 2013, http://cpc.people.com.cn/pinglun/n/2013/0821/c241220-22644745.html.

24. "Core Socialist Values," *China Daily*, October 12, 2017, www.chinadaily.com.cn/china/19thcpcnationalcongress/2017-10/12/content_33160115.htm.

25. Karrie J. Koesel, "Legitimacy, Resilience, and Political Education in Russia and China: Learning to Be Loyal," in Karrie J. Koesel, Valerie J. Bunce, and Jessica Chen Weiss (eds.), *Citizens and the State in Authoritarian Regimes: Comparing China and Russia* (New York: Oxford University Press, 2020), 250–278.

26. "Xi Jinping Thought Added into Curriculum: Ministry of Education," *Global Times*, August 24, 2021; "China's Children Start First Day Schooled in 'Xi Jinping Thought,'" *The Guardian*, September 3, 2021.

27. Xin Li and Kjeld Erik Brødsgaard, "SOE Reform in China: Past, Present and Future," *Copenhagen Journal of Asian Studies* 31, no. 2 (2013): 54–78, https://citeseerx.ist.psu.edu/viewdoc/download?doi=10.1.1.998.1724&rep=rep1&type=pdf.

28. Xi Jinping, "Party Leadership Is the Unique Strength of SOEs," in *The Governance of China* (Beijing: Foreign Language Press, 2017), 2:195.

29. Elizabeth C. Economy, *The Third Revolution: Xi Jinping and the New Chinese State* (New York: Oxford University Press, 2018), 116; Blanchette, *China's New Red Guards*.

30. Xi, "Party Leadership Is the Unique Strength of SOEs," 261.

31. Economy, *The Third Revolution*, 118.

32. "中国抗疫策略强化'国进民退'" [China's pandemic strategy against the epidemic strengthens the state and weakens the people], *Wall Street Journal*, March 23, 2020, https://cn.wsj.com/articles/中国抗疫策略强化"国进民退"-11584591909.

33. Conversations in Hong Kong, October 2018.

34. Michael Clarke, "China's Hidden Totalitarianism," *National Interest*, August 29, 2018, https://nationalinterest.org/feature/chinas-hidden-totalitarianism-29992.

35. Xi, "Tighten Political Activities Within Our Party," 197.

36. Ai Jun, "Why Xinjiang Governance Is Worthy of Copying," *Global Times*, November 28, 2018.

37. Elected legislatures and governments in several Western countries, such as the United States, Canada, the Netherlands, the United Kingdom, and Lithuania have characterized China's treatment of the Muslim Uighurs in Xinjiang as genocide.

38. James McMurray, "The UN's Report on the Uyghurs Nearly Didn't See the Light of Day, Thanks to China," *The Guardian*, September 1, 2022.

39. Stein Ringen, *The Perfect Dictatorship: China in the 21st Century* (Hong Kong: Hong Kong University Press, 2016).

40. Phoebe Zhang, "Cities in China Most Monitored in the World, Report Finds," *South China Morning Post*, August 19, 2019; "中国天网已建成 2亿摄像头毫秒级寻" [China's Skynet has made 200 million cameras for identity searches in milliseconds], *Ifeng*, May 4, 2018, http://tech.ifeng .com/a/20180504/44980719_0.shtml.

41. "解码人脸识别技术：'刷脸'，正走入你我生活" [Face recognition technology decoded: "face scanning" is now part of our lives], *Xinhua*, August 15, 2018, www.xinhuanet.com/2018-08/15/c_1123269994.htm; "'Electronic Police' Is On Guard at Shenzhen's Crossings," *CGTN*, April 17, 2017, https://news.cgtn.com/news/3d51544d77557a4d/share_p.html.

42. "Document 9: A ChinaFile Translation," *ChinaFile*, November 8, 2013, www.chinafile.com/document-9-chinafile-translation#start.

43. "习近平灵机一动 立马改了'三个自信'" [Xi immediately changes "the three self-confidences"], *China News*, December 23, 2014, https//news .creaders.net/china/2014/12/23/1459773.html.

44. Brown, *The World According to Xi*.

45. Xi Jinping, 习近平谈治国理政 [Xi Jinping: the governance of China] (Beijing: Foreign Language Press, 2014), 38.

46. For analyses of the resolution of history, see "Guest #12: History Resolution Lacks History," *China Neican*, December 8, 2021, www.Neican .org/guest-12-history-resolutions-lack-of-history.

47. Hart, "Creating the Cult of Xi Jinping," 4–32.

48. Victor K. Fong, "Imagining the Future from History: The Tang Dynasty and the 'China Dream,'" in Ying-Kit Chan and Fei Chen (eds.), *Alternative Representations of the Past: The Politics of History in Modern China* (Berlin and Boston: De Gruyter Oldenbourg, 2020), 149–172.

49. Elizabeth J. Perry, "Cultural Governance in Contemporary China: 'Re-orienting' Party Propaganda," *Harvard-Yenching Institute Working Papers*, https://dash.harvard.edu/handle/1/11386987.

50. Xi Jinping, "Exchanges and Mutual Learning Make Civilizations Richer and More Colourful," in *The Governance of China* (Beijing: Foreign Language Press, 2014), 1: 285–286, 288.

51. "Xi Stresses Consolidating Sense of Community for Chinese Nation," PR Newswire/CCTV, August 30, 2021, www.prnewswire.com/in /news-releases/xi-stresses-consolidating-sense-of-community-for-chinese -nation-819979270.html.

52. David Tobin, "China Once Celebrated Its Diversity. How Has It Come to Embrace Ethnic Nationalism?," *The Guardian*, December 5, 2020.

53. Ji Yuqiao, "Chinese Vlogger Li Ziqi Once Again Sets Guinness World Record for 'Most Subscribers for a Chinese Language Channel on YouTube,'" *Global Times*, February 2, 2021.

54. Kevin Joseph Carrico, *The Great Han Race, Nationalism, and Tradition in China Today* (Oakland: University of California Press, 2017).

55. "From Cosplay to Cause Play: Why the Communist Party Supports a Revival in Traditional Chinese Clothing," *South China Morning Post*, June 13, 2019.

56. Xi Jinping, "Xi Jinping: Young People Should Practice the Core Socialist Values," in *The Governance of China* (Beijing: Foreign Languages Press, 2014), 1: 185–199.

57. Kerry Brown, "Xi's China and Han Fei: A Lesson in Authority," *openDemocracy*, December 18, 2015, www.opendemocracy.net/en/han-feis -china-shiver-of-authority; Bougon, *Inside the Mind of Xi Jinping*, 122–127; Jianying Zha, "China's Heart of Darkness: Prince Han Fei and Chairman Xi Jinping: Part I: The Dark Prince," *China Heritage*, July 14, 2020, https:// chinaheritage.net/journal/chinas-heart-of-darkness-prince-han-fei-chairman -xi-jinping-part-i.

58. Qin Hui, 传统十论 [On the traditional ten] (Hong Kong: Oriental Press, 2014). See also Zha, "China's Heart of Darkness."

59. "China's Xi Jinping Unveils New 'Four Comprehensives' Slogans," BBC News, February 25, 2015.

60. "今年首批中央文献重要术语'外语版'出炉 共30个" [This year's first batch of foreign language versions of central documents and important conditions is published—thirty in total], *Guancha*, May 4, 2015, www.guancha .cn/culture/2015-05-04-318218-1.shtml.

61. Jamie P. Horsley, "Party Leadership and Rule of Law in the Xi Jinping Era: What Does an Ascendant Chinese Communist Party Mean for China's Legal Development?" Brookings, September 2019, https://law .yale.edu/sites/default/files/area/center/china/document/horsley_china _party-_legal_development.pdf.

62. Trivium China Tip Sheet, December 14, 2020,

63. For a comparison between Hu, Jiang, and Deng, see Neil Thomas, "China Politics 2025: Stronger as China Goes," MacroPolo, October 26, 2020.

64. Halvor Eifring in the podcast *De mektige*. Del 2. "Xi Jinping" [The mighty. Part 2. "Xi Jinping"], NRK Verdibørsen Podkast [Norwegian State Broadcasting Podcast], Value Exchange, January 27, 2022, https://radio.nrk .no/podkast/verdiboersen/l_4aa4d028-d4e9-496c-a4d0-28d4e9696c68.

# 6

# Stepping onto
# the World Stage

"THOSE WHO BULLY CHINA WILL HAVE THEIR HEADS BASHED bloody," thunders Xi Jinping.[1] The contrast to Hu Jintao's talk about China's "Efforts to advance the lofty cause of peace and development for mankind" could hardly be greater.[2] The tone of China's foreign policy may have changed completely, but the content is largely a continuance of that in Hu Jintao's day. For it was on Hu's watch that Beijing began to abandon Deng Xiaoping's cautious line, where domestic development was given priority over foreign influence. Many of Xi's international signature projects are also continuations of strategies launched before. The so-called New Silk Road (Belt and Road) initiative continues strategies previously known as "go out" and "development of the western areas," which date back to the millennium shift. They aimed, respectively, to encourage Chinese companies to invest abroad and speed up economic development in Chinese western provinces.

The assertive foreign policy we see today can be traced back at least to the time of the Beijing Olympics (2008) and the global financial crisis (2008–2009). Beijing tackled both well, which boosted self-confidence in the international arena. That was before Xi became general secretary. Xi thus did not create a break with Chinese foreign policy, but on his watch change has really accelerated. China has come out of the closet as a global great power.

Xi's new, more assertive international line is particularly visible in the style and tone of communication. Xi demands that China gets the global recognition and influence a country of the Middle Kingdom's caliber deserves, and Chinese diplomats follow this up. They speak at the top of their voices, at times in undiplomatic terms, when they defend China and her interests. The rough tone can make diplomatic colleagues from near and far choke on their tea or coffee, while nationalists at home cheer. Gone are the cautious diplomats of Hu's era. They have been replaced by "wolf warriors."

What characterizes the new assertive foreign policy? What can explain this paradigm shift, and how does it affect China's relations with the rest of the world?

## A New Great Power

Once and for all Xi has broken with Deng's cautious line, replacing it with his own "great power diplomacy" (大国外交). At a meeting with President Barack Obama as early as June 2013, Xi, still wet behind his presidential ears, launched the idea of a new type of great power relationship between the two countries. What is new is that in accordance with its increased status and influence, China plays a far more active role on the international stage. Xi repeated his expectations of a bigger say for China in international affairs during the twentieth party congress in October 2022, albeit indirectly, by calling for more diversity and equality in international affairs.[3]

Not least, the country's representatives make themselves heard in international organizations, where they work for China to have an influence more in keeping with its weight.[4] Beijing is not content with adapting to the international system; it wants to shape it and expects Chinese values, interests, and views to have more impact in the United Nations.[5] Chinese authorities not only increasingly use their position in international organizations to exercise influence in international relations but also establish their own international organizations as alternatives to existing ones, as is the case with the Asian Infrastructure Investment Bank.

Furthermore, China takes more responsibility in vital international affairs as befits a global superpower. It aroused as much joy as surprise when China signed the Paris Agreement on Climate Change in 2016 and when Beijing and Washington proclaimed in 2021 that they would strengthen their cooperation on climate issues.[6] While China's previous leaders conducted diplomacy *with* the great powers, Xi's China does diplomacy *as* a great power.[7]

Great power status goes with the fact that China's global footprint has grown. The country is present in all four corners of the globe, and wherever you go today, you meet Chinese people: from the Yellow River research station on Spitsbergen, to the Chinese port in Gwadar in Pakistan and China's first overseas military base in the tiny African country Djibouti, to Chinese research stations among the penguins in the Antarctic. China has the second-largest economy in the world and will surpass the United States to have the world's largest in 2030, according to some forecasts.[8] China is the largest trading partner of at least 120 countries.[9] Beijing also provides, according to some calculations, as much aid to the world's poor as the United States does.[10]

China has also become a great power within research and development. In fact, the country is a world leader in fields such as artificial intelligence, quantum and biotechnology. In March 2021 the Chinese landed on Mars, a huge success for the country's space program.

Furthermore, China has built up a military power that, to an ever-growing degree, has the capacity to support the country's global interests. The Chinese navy's more frequent operation in distant seas is one visible example of that.

Øystein Tunsjø, professor at the Institute for Defence Studies in Oslo, claims that this global shift in power has gone so far in China's favor that we are now getting close to a bipolar world order with China and the United States as rivals for global dominance.[11] Tunsjø's analysis is supported by studies measuring various great powers' influence on other countries. These studies show that China's global influence has increased markedly since the turn of the millennium, primarily at the cost of the United States.[12]

This trend was well under way before Xi came to power. Everything was thus set for a man ambitious for a new global role for

China. Already before he came to power, attentive China observers noticed signals that the aspiring leader would be tough in foreign policy. During a visit to Mexico in 2009, Xi announced, "There are some foreigners who have eaten their fill and have nothing better to do than stick their fingers in our affairs."[13] If someone thought that this lament was the result of jetlag or a bad in-flight meal, they would soon be proven wrong. As newly elected party general secretary, Xi later affirmed that China under his rule would never sacrifice its core interests, warning that China would never "swallow the bitter fruit of damaging China's sovereignty, security, or development interests."[14] A new foreign policy was about to hatch. A tough nationalist had come to the throne of the Middle Kingdom; Deng's cautious policy was ready for the bin.

Under Deng foreign policy had been about avoiding making enemies and lying low in the international terrain. Conflicts with other states were to be avoided, or at any rate postponed.[15] For example, already in 1978 Deng pronounced that the conflicts with Japan should be left for the next generation, which had more wisdom.[16] Twelve years later he formulated the mantra that would steer China's conduct outside its borders: "Observe calmly, secure our positions; cope with affairs calmly; hide our capacities and make some achievements" (冷静观察, 稳住阵脚, 沉着应付, 韬光养晦, 有所作为), known as *Taoguang yanghui*). The young People's Republic was still weak and not very robust, Deng thought; it needed to concentrate on its consolidation and development.[17] For this reason, Beijing only engaged in foreign affairs that directly concerned the country, what were later defined as China's "core interests" (核心利益): (1) China's basic system and national security, (2) national and territorial integrity, and (3) viable economic and social development.[18] Deng's policy served China well for several decades. The country was left to work in peace on securing economic and social development, while other countries greedily observed the business opportunities there.

This cautious line was always meant to be temporary, however: "By the end of the century China will have quadrupled its gross national product and reached a level of comparative prosperity. When that time comes, China will surely play a bigger role in maintaining world peace and stability," promised Deng.[19]

Xi believes that the time has come, and he is keeping Deng's promise. China is in "a period of strategic possibilities" (战略机遇期), affirmed Xi in a speech in 2014.[20] Wisdom and strength are now in place; China is nearing the center of the global stage (走近世界舞台中央) and by 2050 will become a global leader.[21]

## Wolf Warrior Diplomacy

The country's diplomats simply had to keep up. As a natural consequence of China's new position, Xi ordered his diplomats to behave in ways fitting the representatives of a great power.[22] Following Deng's mantra, the Chinese authorities had behaved calmly, tactfully, and restrainedly on the international stage. So boring, dry, and devoid of substance appeared Chinese diplomats that anonymous Chinese are said to have sent calcium pills to the Ministry of Foreign Affairs to show their displeasure at its employees' lack of backbone.[23] This style of diplomacy was inappropriate for a country of China's size and importance, Xi felt, and Chinese diplomats did not need to be asked twice to replace it. Indeed, Chinese diplomats have become so aggressive and confrontational that both foreign observers and Chinese state-owned media use the expression "wolf warrior diplomacy" (战狼外交).[24] The name comes from two patriotic films, *The Wolf Warrior* and *The Wolf Warrior 2*, in which a Rambo-like special forces soldier travels around the world saving Chinese people by defeating American mercenaries.[25] The Chinese have flocked to the cinemas to watch these films. Obviously, Chinese diplomats have stuffed themselves with calcium tablets. They have become wolf warriors and now tackle conflicts out in the open.

An example of this is the behavior of former ambassador to Sweden Gui Congyou. When Swedish Chinese writer and dissident Gui Minhai received the Swedish national Pen Prize in 2019, the ambassador soberly informed the Swedes, "We treat our friends with fine wine, but for our enemies we have shotguns."[26] China's man in Stockholm is in good company. The country's ambassador in Brazil was no less free in his speech when he called the then-president's family "poison" after Jair Bolsonaro's son blamed what he referred to as the Chinese dictatorship for the Covid-19 pandemic. The ambassador to Venezuela told this host country's authorities to "put on a face mask and shut up" after they referred to the "Wuhan virus."[27] Lu Shaye, ambassador to Canada, accused his host country of white supremacist thinking after Huawei's Meng Wanzhou was arrested.[28]

A macabre example of wolf warrior diplomacy is a photograph, most likely photoshopped, of an Australian soldier holding a knife to the throat of an Afghan child. Zhao Lijian, press spokesman for the Chinese Ministry of Foreign Affairs and the high priest of wolf warriors, posted the photo on his Twitter account with the sarcastic caption "Don't be afraid, we are coming to bring you peace."[29] Zhao's target was not just Australia but the whole US-led coalition in Afghanistan and the lack of results for their efforts.

A more passive-aggressive style of Chinese diplomacy is what has been called "diplomacy of indignation": Chinese diplomats arguing that the feelings of the Chinese people are hurt when national interests are harmed.[30] The major Danish newspaper *Jylland Posten* has been on the receiving end of just such an indignant diplomatic response. When it published a cartoon in January 2020 of the Chinese flag with the stars swapped for symbols of the corona virus, the Chinese ambassador in Copenhagen reacted by emphasizing "strong indignation" and that the cartoon had "[hurt] the feelings of the Chinese people."[31] This diplomatic style can be understood as foreign diplomacy's version of emotional blackmail.

Wolf warrior diplomacy has contributed to tensions between China and the United States now being at a historic high. Since the 1970s relations, despite fundamental disagreements, were characterized by both sides realizing that they had too much to gain from cooperating to risk letting conflict escalate out of control. Around 2018 this changed. The disagreements about China's trade surplus with the United States led to a trade war. The United States accused China of unfair trade practices and the theft of intellectual property and imposed customs duties on Chinese exports. China retaliated with duties on US imports that Wall Street analysts described thus: "On a scale of 1–10, it's an 11."[32]

Zhao Lijian managed to get into a Twitter war with former US National Security Advisor Susan Rice despite his being stationed at the other side of the globe. After he claimed that white people never go to the southeastern part of Washington, DC, Rice called him a racist disgrace and demanded he be recalled to Beijing. Zhao returned Rice's "disgrace" and "ignorant" and added "disgusting."[33]

The Covid-19 pandemic worsened the situation. The Donald Trump administration was quick to claim the virus had leaked from a laboratory in Wuhan, calling it "the China virus." As might be expected, Zhao did not let such a claim go unchallenged and introduced the idea that American soldiers had brought the virus to China.[34] Chinese media joined the blame game. In an editorial in May 2020, the Communist party paper the *Global Times* claimed that Washington had made deadly errors, wasted time, and responded too late, thus dragging the world into a longer-lasting pandemic.[35] Readers had to double-check that they had not opened an American paper and misread "Washington" for "Beijing", because the claims were almost identical to those the Trump administration was making about the way Beijing had tackled the virus.

Chinese state news bureau Xinhua reacted to the American accusations in a more humorous way with a short animated film titled "Once Upon a Virus." It shows a quarrel between two Lego-like figures representing the American and Chinese sides, making fun of what the filmmakers think are the United States' double standards, self-contradictions, and unreasonable accusations.[36] Out of the mouth of the American figure bubble phrases that are particularly provoking for Chinese nationalists, such as "Typical third world" and "Look how backward China is!" The cartoon thus fires up anti-American feelings among the Chinese.

From a respectful relationship, or at least a mutual understanding of the advantage of appearing respectful, Chinese-US relations have deteriorated into open confrontation and competition.

## An Elephant Cannot Hide Behind a Little Tree

"The cake was also decorated with a fake flag" was part of Foreign Ministry spokesperson Zhao Lijian's explanation of why a librarian at the Taipei Trade Office in Fiji ended up with a concussion after a tussle with a Chinese diplomat.[37] During the celebration of Taiwan's national day in Fiji's capital, Suva, in 2020, uninvited representatives from the Chinese embassy turned up and photographed the guests. To their horror, they caught sight of a cake decorated with the Taiwanese flag. When the disgruntled Chinese were asked to leave, the affair ended in a melee, and the Taiwanese librarian went to the hospital with a head injury. The fact that the Chinese diplomats felt so offended, largely by a cake decoration, that they resorted to violence to defend their country's honor speaks volumes about the insecurity that still characterizes the new superpower.

For journalist and author Peter Martin, this combination of self-confidence and insecurity explains China's wolf warrior diplomacy. China as a great power in general and Chinese diplomats in particular are, on the one hand, arrogant, sure of themselves, and self-righteous; on the other, they are fragile, insecure, and nervous.[38] Without a doubt national confidence has grown with the economy and China's expanding presence abroad over the past forty years. The Communist Party newspaper the *People's Daily* points to the country's size to explain why China stands tall on the international stage: "An elephant cannot hide behind a little tree."[39] With the world's biggest population, its second-biggest economy, and the biggest standing armed forces, China naturally should have a greater global influence.

Self-confidence and a more assertive and confrontational line thus did not start under Xi but can be traced back at least as far as the Beijing Olympics of 2008. This successful event was both a source of national pride and a personal triumph for Xi, who was in overall charge of the games. The gunpowder smoke had scarcely cleared (literally, for the dazzling opening ceremony showcased China's four great inventions) before the global financial crisis struck. China too was affected: in 2009 its economic growth, after having increased steadily for the past decade, slowed, but it recovered faster than the Western economies. In 2010 China overtook Japan as the world's second-largest economy. All this strengthened the confidence of the Chinese Communist Party and the belief that the Chinese system of government was superior to that of Western countries.

At the same time China is characterized by national insecurity. As a former Chinese ambassador to France pointed out, "You need to be thick skinned to be a superpower—a characteristic which the Chinese people lack."[40] The Chinese authorities, painfully aware that internal problems threaten the country's stability, are paranoid about how the rest of the world, particularly the West, handles China. Many in China, politicians and ordinary people alike, believe other countries are ganging up to encircle and contain China.[41] This anxiety was reflected in Xi Jinping's opening speech at of the twentieth party congress in 2022. Xi did indeed repeat the traditional and optimistic characterization of the presence as a period of "strategic opportunity," but he painted a more nuanced picture by also describing it as a period "in which strategic opportunities, risks, and challenges are concurrent and uncertainties and unforeseen factors are rising."[42]

Beijing feels that traditional diplomacy will not work against such hostility from the outside world. The Chinese perceive representatives of other states as aggressive, self-centered, unwilling to compromise, impolite, and largely ignorant of other perspectives—and they pay them back in same coin.

This combination of vulnerability and self-confidence is a central component of Chinese nationalism. The vulnerability comes from the idea that from the 1840s on, the West imposed a "century of humiliation" on China, robbing it of its rightful place as a global great power. The self-confidence comes from its being on the way to recovering this lost position.

Nationalism is a strong force that influences foreign policy and shapes its wolf warrior diplomacy.[43] Nationalist campaigns that aimed to strengthen support for the Communist Party in the population have created nationalists who cannot tolerate the authorities budging an inch in conflicts with other states.[44] If they do, the nationalists might turn against them. During the violent anti-Japanese demonstrations in 2012 and 2013, for instance, the demonstrators were angry not just with the Japanese but also with the Chinese authorities, whom they thought too lenient with Tokyo.[45] In such situations nationalists lash out at the Ministry of Foreign Affairs in particular, which they gladly call the "Ministry of National Treason" (卖国部).[46] Promoting Chinese interests in an aggressive manner had thus been a way of securing nationalist goodwill even before Xi came to power. Wolf warrior diplomacy is welcomed by nationalist

Chinese, who, according to the Ministry of Foreign Affairs's clearly satisfied management, are sending ever fewer calcium pills.[47]

Therefore, many developments in China prepared the way for a more assertive line even before Xi took over. But he has put a tiger in the tank, as the old Esso advertisement boasted. Xi has been far clearer than his predecessors, both in word and in deed, about ambitions for a bigger and bolder place for China in the world. An example is the speech Xi gave to the Politburo in May 2021, in which he underlined how vital it was to strengthen China's influence in international communications to shape world opinion.[48] Beijing wants to steer international debates in a more China-friendly direction.

Xi has also seen to it that the message of increased Chinese international influence reaches its diplomats. In July 2020 the Ministry of Foreign Affairs established the Centre for the Study of Xi's Thoughts on Diplomacy.[49] Xi also sent a handwritten letter to his diplomats in 2019 with a clear challenge: show greater fighting spirit![50]

In addition, Xi has taken steps to strengthen the power of the Ministry of Foreign Affairs. Traditionally, the ministry's status and budget have been low compared to those of other countries' foreign ministries, but during his first term, Xi almost doubled its budget.[51] While many countries are cutting their diplomatic representation, China was expanding its, and in 2019 it surpassed the United States in the number of stations abroad.[52]

Xi has also raised the status and influence of the Ministry of Foreign Affairs. In 2018 he promoted Foreign Minister Wang Yi to state councilor while allowing him to retain his post as foreign minister.[53] Wang had defended his wolf warriors by affirming that China would always hit back against malicious slanders and defend its honor and interests.[54] This new, elevated status for the foreign minister was also given to Wang's successor, Qin Gang, in March 2023.[55] In this way, the foreign minister now holds one of ten seats at the prime minister's table, the State Council, becoming one of the Prime Minister's close advisors. During a press conference after the National People's Congress in 2023, just days assuming the post of state councilor, Qin issued a warning to Washington, DC: "Containment and suppression will not make America great."[56] Any remaining doubt as to whether Qin is a wolf warrior was cast aside at his answer to just that question: "Now that I have come back to be the foreign minister, and the title [of Wolf Warrior] is no longer given to me, I really feel like I have lost something."[57]

Xi has not only enabled the Ministry of Foreign Affairs to execute his foreign ambitions by providing it with economic means and political clout. With demands of absolute loyalty and sanctions for the least deviation, he has also created motivation for doing so through fear in individual diplomats. Xi has institutionalized paranoia in the Communist Party,[58] a paranoia that embraces the Ministry of Foreign Affairs. Peter Martin points out that anxious diplomats secure themselves against sanctions by pursuing a line that is as assertive as or even more so than Xi's to show their obedience to his strategy.[59] This dynamic is an example of a trend throughout the history of the People's Republic: when a strong leader demands obedience and discipline, the country's diplomats become a pack of easily offended (on the nation's behalf) watchdogs.

The wolf warrior diplomats are driven not just by fear but also by career ambitions. The kind of straight talking described here has proved a good way to advance one's career. Performance appraisals now measure diplomats by their PR activities.[60] So it pays to be tough in conflicts with your host country.

The previously mentioned Zhao Lijian is a shining example. With a million followers on Twitter and several fan pages on social media, he was welcomed back as a hero when he returned from Pakistan in 2019.[61] Both his superiors and the population at large liked the Twitter war he had waged against former US National Security Advisor Susan Rice. Zhao's career soared. He succeeded Hua Chunying as deputy director of the Ministry of Foreign Affairs' Information Department when Hua was promoted to director.[62]

Hua herself was known for her straight and tough replies to foreign journalists. When she likened Mike Pompeo to "Auntie Xianglin," the international public at first found the comparison more confusing than striking. You need to know your Lu Xun, China's national author, to know that "Auntie Xianglin" is a pitiable, fussy, nagging character in a novel who keeps on telling the same story over and over. A final example is Lu Shaye, ambassador to Canada, who accused his host country of white supremacist thinking. He was awarded with a direct flight from Ottawa to Paris, a promotion, given France's permanent seat on the UN Security Council.[63]

So, in many cases, the domestic public, from Xi Jinping at the top to the nationalist next door, is the wolf warriors' target. And they are far more worried about being seen as weak at home than about harming China's international reputation.[64]

## The Backlash

The Pew Research Center in Washington, DC, publishes information about social conditions both in the United States and globally. It has surveyed what people in seventeen countries in Europe, North America, and the Pacific region think about China and found that views on China and its authorities are now at a historic low. It is perhaps not surprising that three out of four Americans and almost nine out of ten Japanese have a negative opinion, but even in Sweden eight out of ten opinions are negative.[65] In China results of domestic research were just as depressing. The China Institutes of Contemporary Relations (CICIR), a think tank connected to the Ministry of State Security (MSS), reports that the anti-Chinese mood in the world has not been stronger since the Tiananmen Square protests in 1989.[66]

The hard rhetoric of the wolf warriors cannot take all the blame for this fall in popularity. Beijing's policies and actions, both in and outside the country, are often disliked outside China. China has deprived Hong Kong of the autonomy it enjoyed under "one country, two systems," despite the fact that this system had served the mainland well. In the West many have long-term bonds with the city, and they reacted strongly to Beijing's tightening grip. The hope that "one country, two systems" could entice Taiwan into a peaceful reunification vanishes with every Hong Konger arrested under the new security law. In Xinjiang Province the authorities have abandoned the policy of accepting ethnic and religious differences that applied for most of the People's Republic's history. Today the authorities hold the province in an iron grip, oppressing and interning Uighurs on an alarming scale.

The Covid-19 pandemic has also played its part in weakening China's international reputation. The Chinese authorities have boasted of how uniquely effective they have been in stopping the pandemic —no other country welded its citizens into their homes—and of how they provided half the world with infection-protection gear. Outside China though, many blame China for the pandemic on account of the authorities allegedly initially keeping the outbreak secret from the world.

In *Xi Jinping: The Backlash*, Richard McGregor of the Lowy Institute in Sydney shows how Xi's policies are meeting opposition. Outside China's borders, the most significant—and for China, the most distressing—trend is that other states are coming together to limit China's growing international influence.[67] The White House needs hardly lift a finger to line up other states, including China's neighbors, in its front against the Middle Kingdom. When heads of state from Germany, Australia, Japan, and the United States meet, it rarely takes long before someone says, "We need to talk about China."[68]

When the United States, Australia, and the United Kingdom agreed on a new trilateral security pact (AUKUS) in September 2021, there was little doubt that the real aim was to limit Beijing's growth and power.[69] The fact that none of the heads of state mentioned China when the pact was announced cannot be interpreted in any other way than as evidence that China was the elephant in the virtual press conference room. This alliance comes on top of the United States breathing life into its "quadrilateral dialogue" with India, Australia, and Japan, and India and Japan both building up their bilateral military cooperation with the United States.[70] China is the common denominator in all of this. Few things are more unifying than a common enemy. The oft-repeated Chinese claim of a policy of encirclement and containment has become a self-fulfilling prophecy.

In 1971, in all secrecy, Henry Kissinger went to the Communist giant in the East. There he did the legwork for the two countries to reconnect after twenty-three years. He claims to have visited there almost a hundred times and is known to be one of China's best friends in the United States. In 2001 Kissinger predicted that the United States would become isolated if Washington named China as the enemy because of its growing economy and its distasteful ideology.[71] Twenty years later the opposite has proven true: other states flock to the United States to join in a common front against China.

The European Union, often deeply divided on foreign policy, now sees the need to come together and decide on a common line toward China.[72] This is probably due to a combination of fear of increased Chinese global interest and displeasure with certain developments inside China. In March 2021 the union passed sanctions against China as a reaction to breaches of human rights in Xinjiang.[73] These were the first joint European sanctions against China since 1989, when the authorities sent in troops to squash the demonstrators in Tiananmen Square. The sanctions thus say a lot about the depth of anti-Chinese sentiment in the union today.

It is not just foreigners who react against wolf warrior diplomacy. High-ranking Chinese diplomat veterans, academics, and military officials are also critical of the new diplomatic style. Fu Ying, for instance, is concerned about international perceptions of China in general and its diplomacy in particular and indirectly warns against aggressive rhetoric from Chinese actors. As deputy foreign minister she was known as someone who could be tough in promoting China's interests in international negotiations, and she was popular with the political elite in Beijing. So it is worth noting when someone like her says that representatives of the authorities must communicate in the same tone as their foreign colleagues to make China more attractive to the outside world. She advises her former colleagues to be humble and inclusive and to use a plain, down-to-earth narrative style—a swipe at the wolf warriors.[74]

As one who shares Fu's opinion, Zhu Feng, director of the Institute of International Relations at the University of Nanjing, reminds us that diplomacy is the art of persuasion and should not be about lashing out at each other (怒怼).[75] Similarly, Shi Zhan of China Foreign Affairs University, often called "the cradle of Chinese diplomats," claims that aggressive pronouncements from Chinese diplomats damage the country's industry more than the Covid pandemic has done.[76] Shi Yinhong, professor of international relations at the prestigious Renmin University in Beijing, points out that the aggressive style in no way achieves what it intends, and he warns against making enemies for China.[77]

Several others warn that China is boxing in the wrong weight class. General Dai Xu, otherwise known as a hawk in questions related to the United States, admonishes his country to dampen its tone as China is still weaker than the United States. If China wishes to surpass and take the place of the United States, it must hide these ambitions from Washington.[78] Deng Pufang, Deng Xiaoping's son, a paraplegic after being tortured and thrown out a window during the Cultural Revolution, asks the Chinese authorities to keep a sober mind and know their place.[79]

The political influence nationalism has gained is another source of worry. Among those concerned is Yan Xuetong, dean of Tsinghua University, one of China's foremost theoreticians within international relations. He argues that Chinese diplomacy must be rational.[80] Former ambassador and party secretary at China's Foreign Affairs University Yuan Nansheng is even more worried and warns that when foreign policy is kidnapped by popular opinion, disaster is inevitable.[81]

Common among all these objections and correctives is that they come from people of experience, who came up under Deng with his cautious approach at a time when China was much weaker. The younger segment, on the contrary, has grown up in the nationalist atmosphere of a fledgling great power and received diplomatic training based on Xi's assertive foreign politics.

Obviously, wolf warrior diplomacy has its price, but it has achieved at least two of its goals. First, the aggressive style has a "self-disciplining" effect on other states. It is not hard to find examples of governments that tiptoe warily in matters where the Chinese authorities have drawn a red line, indirectly or directly. Second, seen from Beijing, the domestic public is as important an audience as the foreign. And aggressive pronouncements on international issues are popular with domestic nationalists.

A speech Xi gave in June 2021 engendered speculation among China analysts about whether a new foreign policy was coming. In his speech he instructed his diplomats to be "more modest and humbler . . . credible, amiable, and respectable." Was China about to return to Deng's cautious foreign policy? If you read the remainder of the speech, the answer is clearly no. For there we can read such familiar notions as that of China "nearing the centre of the global stage," that China shall contribute more "to solving humanity's problems," and that China "opposes unilateralism and hegemony."[82]

So the foreign policy goals remain the same: increased international influence. Xi's opening speech during the twentieth party congress in October 2022 emphasized diversity and equality in international affairs, code for greater Chinese international influence.

However, Xi probably realizes that the aggressive style has had negative side effects and does not accomplish what it was designed for. Peter Martin calls it a change in tactics but not in strategy.[83] Perhaps Xi recognizes that the wolf warrior style is not the best—or at least not the only—way to achieve his foreign policy goals. Soft power is also important for promoting Chinese interests.

## Conclusion

The West's view of China has shifted between what we in our book *49 Myths About China* call "Sinophilia" and "Sinophobia" for as long as there has been an awareness in the West of the great country in the East.[84] Over the past decade we have seen that Sinophobia is spreading in the West. Pew's survey of attitudes to China, mentioned earlier in this chapter, clearly shows this.

Negative perceptions are not necessarily without foundation. There is much cause for concern in developments in Xi's China: the authoritarian trend, rearmament, and an ever more assertive attitude in international affairs. The less-than-amiable wolf warriors also contribute greatly to negative perceptions about China.

Nonetheless such negative attitudes sometimes fall into the category of myths rather than truths. Old prejudices about China and the Chinese, summed up by the cliché "the yellow peril," have once more become fashionable at the same time as new ones have popped up. In *The Long Game: China's Grand Strategy to Displace American Order*, Rush Doshi, one of President Joe Biden's most prominent China advisors, writes that China plans no less than world domination by 2040. In this plan the United States is reduced to "a deindustrialized, English-speaking version of a Latin American republic" that subsists on transnational tax evasion.[85]

Ordinary Americans also harbor ideas that the Chinese have many frightening plans. "They are scary as their government thinks in hundred-year plans and our government thinks in four-year plans," and they are "highly intelligent and very innovative."[86] Not only has the hope of a democratic development in China vanished, but many also now fear that China will impose its authoritarian form of government on the rest of the world. Statements such as the Chinese aim "to overtake the United States in world dominance [and] also want to destroy democracy"[87] and "Beijing is trying to convince the global community that authoritarian systems are better than democracies"[88] sum up this fear.

Many myths reveal as much about how we see ourselves as they do about China.[89] That China's growth nurtures our fears of scary plans of global dominance reflects our fears of our own vulnerability in Europe and the United States. The idea that China is buying up the whole world falls on fertile ground not just because the country has money in the bank and is on a buying spree but also because so many Western economies are struggling with the long-term consequences of the financial crisis and the Covid pandemic. That fear of the Chinese imposing their authoritarian form of governance on the rest of the world resonates might have more to do with Americans' and Europeans' weakened faith in their democracies than with any existing plans in Zhongnanhai. The mob's storming of Congress in Washington makes it difficult to take US democracy for granted or see it as infallible.

An unfortunate symbiosis occurs between negative myths and the wolf warriors' verbal shotgun shooting. This aggravates alienation and hostility, an "us" versus "them" feeling. We have long seen the contours of a new cold war between East and West.

## Notes

1. "习近平：谁妄想欺负中国必将碰得头破血流" [Xi Jinping: those who bully China will have their heads bashed bloody], *Yifeng*, June 1, 2021, https://news.ifeng.com/c/87W3OzVDDs2.

2. Hu Jintao, "Make Joint Efforts to Advance the Lofty Cause of Peace and Development for Mankind," *China Daily*, December 31, 2007, https://www.chinadaily.com.cn/china/2007-12/31/content_6361877.htm

3. "Transcript: President Xi Jinping's Report to China's 2022 Party Congress," *Nikkei*, October 18, 2022, https://asia.nikkei.com/Politics/China

-s-party-congress/Transcript-President-Xi-Jinping-s-report-to-China-s
-2022-party-congress.

4. Stephen N. Smith, "China's 'Major Country Diplomacy': Legitimation and Foreign Policy Change," *Foreign Policy Analysis* 17, no. 2 (2021), https://academic.oup.com/fpa/article/17/2/orab002/6139347.

5. Xi Jinping, "China's Diplomacy Must Befit Its Major-Country Status," in *The Governance of China* (Beijing: Foreign Language Press, 2017), 2: 479–483; Avery Goldstein, "China's Grand Strategy Under Xi Jinping: Reassurance, Reform, and Resistance," *International Security* 45, no. 1 (2020): 164–201, https://direct.mit.edu./isec/article-abstract/45/1/164/95252/Chin-s -Grand-Strategy-under-Xi-Jinping.

6. "China Signs Paris Agreement on Climate Change," State Council, People's Republic of China, February 23, 2016, http://english.www.gov.cn /state_council/vice_premiers/2016/04/23/content_281475333331232.htm; "COP26: China and US Agree to Boost Climate Co-operation," BBC, November 11, 2021.

7. Kato Yoshikazu, "What Is Xi Jinping's Major Power Diplomacy?" *Asia Global Online*, March 7, 2019, https://www.asiaglobalonline.hku.hk/xi -jinping-china-major-power-diplomacy

8. "World Economic League table," Centre for Economics and Business Research, December 26, 2021, https://cebr.com/service/macroeconomic -forecasting.

9. Iman Ghosh, "How China Overtook the U.S. as the World's Major Trading Partner," *Visual Capitalist*, January 22, 2020, www.visualcapitalist .com/china-u-s-worlds-trading-partner.

10. Nancy Qian, "The Case for Chinese Foreign Aid," *Project Syndicate*, November 8, 2021.

11. Øystein Tunsjø, *The Return of Bipolarity in World Politics* (New York: Columbia University Press), 2018.

12. Jonathan D. Moyer et al., "China-US Competition: Measuring Global Influence," Atlantic Council, May 2021, www.atlanticcouncil.org /wp-content/uploads/2021/06/China-US-Competition-Report-2021.pdf.

13. "中国要输出革命折腾世界，李克强两大峰会重点宣扬习近平思想" [China will export revolution to turn the world upside down, Li Keqiang focuses on spreading Xi Jinping's ideas at top meetings], *Zhongguo xinwen zhongxin*, November 2, 2019, https://chinanewscenter.com/archives/15466.

14. Dean Cheng, "China's Xi Jinping's New Hard Line and the U.S.-Japan Alliance," Heritage Foundation, February 12, 2013, https://www.heritage.org /asia/report/chinas-xi-jinpings-new-hard-line-and-the-us-japan-alliance.

15. Ezra F. Vogel, *Deng Xiaoping and the Transformation of China* (Cambridge, MA: Belknap Press of Harvard University Press, 2011), 713.

16. Chikako Kawakatsu Ueki, "Liberal Deterrence of China: Challenges in Achieving Japan's China Policy," in Takashi Inoguchi, G. John Ikenberry,

and Yoichiro Sato (eds.), *The U.S.-Japan Security Alliance: Regional Multi-lateralism* (New York: Palgrave Macmillan, 2011).

17. Chas W. Freeman Jr., "China's National Experiences and the Evolution of PRC Grand Strategy," in David Shambaugh (ed.), *China and the World* (New York: Oxford University Press, 2020), 46; Wang Hongying, "From 'Taoguang Yanghui' to 'Yousuo Zuowei': China's Engagement in Financial Minilateralism," *CIGI Papers* 52 (2014): 1, www.cigionline.org/sites/default /files/cigi_paper_no52.pdf.

18. Dai Bingguo, then foreign minister, defined China's core interests in 2009: "中国为什么要宣示核心利益?" [Why should China announce its core interests?], *Sohu*, July 28, 2010, http://news.sohu.com/20100728/n 273816207.shtml. Later the Chinese authorities specified and expanded these core interests, among other things, by explicitly including Taiwan, Tibet, Xinjiang, and Hong Kong. The Chinese authorities have drawn red lines around these interests, and these red lines still apply.

19. Deng Xiaoping, "Peace and Development Are the Two Outstanding Issues in the World Today," Selected Works of Deng Xiaoping, March 4, 1985, https://dengxiaopingworks.wordpress.com/2013/03/18/peace-and -development-are-the-two-outstanding-issues-in-the-world-today.

20. "中央外事工作会议在京举行 习近平发表重要讲话" [The central conference on work related to foreign affairs was held in Beijing. Xi Jinping held an important speech], *Zhongguo Gongchandang xinwen*, November 8, 2014, http://cpc.people.com.cn/n/2014/1130/c64094-26119225.html.

21. Martin, *China's Civilian Army*, 212.

22. Xi Jinping, "Xi Jinping: China's Diplomacy Must Befit Its Major-Country Status," in *The Governance of China II* (Beijing: Foreign Languages Press, 2017), 481–483.

23. Huang Lan Lan, "Young Chinese Idolize FM Spokespersons, Welcome 'Wolf Warrior' Diplomats," *Global Times*, May 21, 2020.

24. See, for example, the state-controlled newspaper *Global Times* defend "the wolf warriors": "West Feels Challenged by China's New 'Wolf Warrior' Diplomacy," *Global Times*, April 16, 2020.

25. Wu Jing, *Wolf Warrior* (战狼), 2015; *Wolf Warrior* 2 (战狼 2), 2017.

26. "How Sweden Copes with Chinese Bullying," *The Economist*, February 22, 2020.

27. Bethany Allen-Ebrahimian, "China's 'Wolf Warrior Diplomacy' Comes to Twitter," *Axios*, April 22, 2020.

28. "China's Ambassador Accuses Canada of 'White Supremacy' in Huawei CFO Arrest," *The Guardian*, January 9, 2019.

29. The picture has been removed from Zhao's Twitter account but is reproduced here: Katie Burgess and Lucy Bladen, "Chinese Digitally Altered Picture of Soldier 'Repugnant': Scott Morrison," *Canberra Times*, updated November 30, 2020.

30. Andreas B. Forsby at the Nordic Institute for Asia Studies has created this concept; Andreas B. Forsby, "What Is Behind China's Diplomacy of Indignation?" *The Diplomat*, November 13, 2020.

31. "Statement by Spokesperson of the Chinese Embassy in Denmark," Embassy of the People's Republic of China in the Kingdom of Denmark, January 27, 2020, http://dk.china-embassy.gov.cn/eng/zdgx/202001/t2020 0128_2557543.htm.

32. Michael Sheetz, "Rating China's Retaliation in the Trade War: 'On a Scale of 1–10, It's an 11,'" CNBC, August 5, 2019.

33. Iain Marlow and Li Dandan, "'You Are a Racist Disgrace': Former National Security Advisor Susan Rice Chides 'Ignorant' Diplomat on Twitter," *Time Magazine*, July 15, 2015, https://time.com/5626551/susan-rice-twitter -chinese-diplomat.

34. Ben Westcott and Steven Jiang, "Chinese Diplomat Promotes Conspiracy Theory That U.S. Military Brought Coronavirus to Wuhan," CNN, March 14, 2020.

35. Chen Qingqing and Leng Shumei, "US Owes World an Explanation on COVID-19," *Global Times*, May 6, 2020.

36. Tracey Shelton and Iris Zhao, "Chinese State Media Releases Animated Propaganda Video Mocking US Coronavirus Response," ABC News, May 1, 2020.

37. "台方贼喊捉贼!" [The Taiwanese thief calls catch the thief!], *Sina*, October 19, 2020, https://news.sina.cn/2020-10-19/detail-iiznctk c6454722.d.html; Will Glasgow, "China Blames Flag Cake as Diplomats Brawl with Taiwan Embassy Staff," *The Australian*, October 20, 2020.

38. Peter Martin, *China's Civilian Army* (New York: Oxford University Press, 2021).

39. "美国挑起贸易战的实质是什么?" [What is the substance of the USA's provocation of a trade war], *Renmin ribao*, August 9, 2018, http:// politics.people.com.cn/n1/2018/0809/c1001-30220090.html.

40. Chen Jian, quoted in Martin, *China's Civilian Army*, 228.

41. See, for example, Catherine Wong, "Beijing Blasts US, Japan for 'Anti-China Encirclement' After Tokyo Talks," *South China Morning Post*, March 17, 2021.

42. "Transcript: President Xi Jinping's Report to China's 2022 Party Congress," *Nikkei*.

43. Peter Hays Gries, "Nationalism, Social Influences, and Chinese Foreign Policy," in David Shambaugh (ed.), *China and the World* (New York: Oxford University Press, 2020), 63–84; Zhao Suisheng, "Foreign Policy Implications of Chinese Nationalism Revisited: The Strident Turn," *Journal of Contemporary China* 22, no. 82 (2013): 535–553; Jessica Chen Weiss,

"How Hawkish Is the Chinese Public? Another Look at 'Rising Nationalism' and Chinese Foreign Policy," *Journal of Contemporary China* 28, no. 119 (2019).

44. Ali Wyne and Ryan Hass, "China's Diplomacy Is Limiting Its Own Ambition," *Foreign Policy*, June 9, 2021.

45. Peter Hays Gries, Derek Steiger, and Tao Wang, "Popular Nationalism and China's Japan Policy: The Diaoyu Islands Protests, 2012–2013," *Journal of Contemporary China* 25, no. 98 (2016).

46. Thomas J. Christensen, "More Actors, Less Coordination? New Challenges for the Leaders for a Rising China," in Gilbert Rozman (ed.), *China's Foreign Policy: Who Makes It, and How Is It Made?* (New York: Palgrave Macmillan, 2012), 29–30.

47. "外交部领导：给外交部寄钙片的人越来越少了" [The Foreign Ministry leadership: fewer and fewer people are sending calcium tablets to the Foreign Ministry], *Guancha*, December 9, 2014.

48. "习近平在中共中央政治局第三十次集体学习时强调 加强和改进国际传播工作 展示真实立体全面的中国" [During the thirtieth collective study session of the Communist Party's Central Committee's Standing Committee Xi Jinping emphasized strengthening and improving international communications work and showing a true, three-dimensional and holistic China], *Xinhua*, June 1, 2021.

49. "Xi Jinping Thought on Diplomacy Research Center Inaugurated," *Xinhua*, July 20, 2020.

50. *Foreign Policy*, August 10, 2021.

51. "China Government Expenditure: Diplomacy," CEIC Data, www.ceicdata.com/en/china/government-revenue-and-expenditure/government-expenditure-diplomacy.

52. "China Spends $12bn More to Extend Its International Influence," Australian Centre on China in the World, Australian National University, March 14, 2018, http://ciw.anu.edu.au/news-and-events/news/china-spends-12bn-more-extend-its-international-influence; Bonnie Bley, "World Diplomacy Stocktake: A Shifting of the Ranks," Lowy Institute, November 27, 2019, www.lowyinstitute.org/the-interpreter/world-diplomacy-stocktake-shifting-ranks.

53. Christian Shepherd, "China Makes 'Silver Fox' Top Diplomat, Promoted to State Councillor," Reuters, March 19, 2018

54. Wendy Wu, "Chinese Foreign Minister Wang Yi Defends 'Wolf Warrior' Diplomats for Standing Up to 'Smears,'" *South China Morning Post*, May 24, 2020.

55. "秦刚任国务委员" [Qin Gang as State Councilor], Ministry of Foreign Affairs of the People's Republic of China, March 12, 2023, https://www.fmprc.gov.cn/wjbzhd/202303/t20230312_11039387.shtml.

56. "外交部长秦刚就中国外交政策和对外关系回答中外记者提问, [Foreign Minister Qin Gang Answers Questions from Chinese and Foreign Journalists on China's Foreign Policy and External Relations], Ministry of Foreign Affairs of the People's Republic of China, March 7, 2023, https://www.mfa.gov.cn/web/wjbzhd/202303/t20230307_11037046.shtml.

57. *Op. cit*

58. Jude Blanchette, "Xi's Gamble," *Foreign Affairs*, July/August 2021.

59. Martin, *China's Civilian Army*, 8–10.

60. Dylan M. H. Loh, "Over Here, Overbearing: The Origins of China's 'Wolf Warrior' Style Diplomacy," *Hong Kong Free Press*, June 12, 2020, https://hongkongfp.com/2020/06/12/over-here-overbearing-the-origins-of-chinas-wolf-warrior-style-diplomacy/.

61. Zhao's Twitter profile: https://twitter.com/zlj517; Keith Zhai and Yew Lun Tian, "In China, a Young Diplomat Rises as Aggressive Foreign Policy Takes Root," March 31, 2020, www.reuters.com/article/us-china-diplomacy-insight/in-china-a-young-diplomat-rises-as-aggressive-foreign-policy-takes-root-idUSKBN21I0F8.

62. Yue Huairang, "赵立坚出任外交部新闻司副司长" [Zhao Lijian appointed vice director of the Information Department of the Foreign Ministry], *The Paper*, August 23, 2019, www.thepaper.cn/newsDetail_forward_4236108; "China's Foreign Ministry Spokeswoman Hua Chunying Promoted to Department Head," *CGTN*, June 22, 2019, https://news.cgtn.com/news/2019-07-22/China-s-FM-spokeswoman-Hua-Chunying-promoted-to-department-head-IxiFNBXmhO/index.html.

63. Keegan Elmer, "China's 'Outspoken' Lu Shaye Leaves Canada to Become Ambassador to France," *South China Morning Post*, August 9, 2019.

64. Martin, *China's Civilian Army*, 9.

65. Laura Silver, "China's International Image Remains Broadly Negative as Views of the U.S. Rebound," Pew Research Center, June 30, 2021.

66. "Internal Chinese Report Warns Beijing Faces Tiananmen-Like Global Backlash over Virus," Reuters, May 4, 2020.

67. Richard McGregor, *Xi Jinping: The Backlash* (Melbourne: Penguin Random House Books, 2019).

68. McGregor, *Xi Jinping*, 98.

69. Tom McTague, "Joe Biden's New World Order," *The Atlantic*, September 16, 2021.

70. Jagannath P. Panda and Eerishika Pankaj, "Xi Jinping, the US-China Rivalry and Beijing's Post-COVID Manoeuvres," in Arthur S. Ding and Jagannath P. Panda (ed.), *Chinese Politics and Foreign Policy Under Xi Jinping* (New York: Routledge, 2021), 220; Drew Hinshaw, Sha Hua, and Laurence Norman, "Pushback on Xi's Vision for China Spreads Beyond U.S.," *Wall Street Journal*, December 28, 2020; McGregor, *Xi Jinping*, 80–81.

71. Henry Kissinger, *Does America Need a Foreign Policy? Toward a Diplomacy for the 21st Century* (New York: Simon & Schuster, 2001), 135.

72. Earl Wang, "How Will the EU Answer China's Turn Toward 'Xi Jinping Thought on Diplomacy'?" *The Diplomat*, July 30, 2020.

73. "EU Agrees First Sanctions on China in More Than 30 Years," *Euronews*, March 22, 2021.

74. Fu Ying, "Shape Global Narratives for Telling Chinas Stories," *Global Times*, April 21, 2020.

75. "疫后中国将领导世界？时殷弘：相反，中国应战略收缩" [Should China lead the world after the pandemic? Shi Yinhong: On the contrary, China ought to hold back strategically], Chongyang Institute for Financial Studies, July 28, 2020,.

76. "北大博士外交学院教授：'战狼'误国" [Doctor at the University in Beijing, professor at China's Foreign Affairs University: "the wolf warriors damage the country"], *China Business Focus*, April 28, 2020, www.cbfau .com/appxg/cbf-201587830.html.

77. "疫后中国将领导世界？" [Should China lead the world after the pandemic?], Chongyang Institute for Financial Studies; Catherine Wong, "Too Soon, Too Loud: Chinese Foreign Policy Advisers Tell 'Wolf Warrior' Diplomats to Tone It Down," *South China Morning Post*, May 14, 2020.

78. Dai Xu, "2020对美国的4个想不到与10个新认识" [Four unexpected things and ten new understandings about the USA in 2020], *Guancha*, July 8, 2020, https://user.guancha.cn/main/content?id=342787.

79. Jun Mai, "Deng Xiaoping's Son Urges China to 'Know Its Place' and Not Be 'Overbearing,'" *South China Morning Post,* October 30, 2018.

80. Wong, "Too Soon, Too Loud."

81. Yuan Nansheng, "资深外交官 袁南生：疫情改变世界秩序，防止发生战略误判" [Senior diplomat Yuan Nansheng: The pandemic changes the world order and prevents strategic mistakes], 163.com, May 3, 2020, www .163.com/dy/article/FBNBCQGN0514C8IB.html.

82. "习近平在中共中央政治局第三十次集体学习时强调 加强和改进国际传播工作 展示真实立体全面的中国" [During the thirtieth collective study session of China's Communist Party's Politburo, Xi Jinping underlined strengthening and improving international communications work and presenting a true, three-dimensional and holistic view of China], *Xinhua*.

83. Quoted in Bill Birtles, "Xi Jinping Hints at a Shift in China's 'Wolf Warrior' Diplomacy. But Does This Mean We'll See a Change in Relations with Australia?" ABC News, June 4, 2021.

84. Stig Stenslie and Marte Kjær Galtung, *49 Myths About China* (Lanham, MD: Rowman & Littlefield, 2015).

85. Rush Doshi, *The Long Game: China's Grand Strategy to Displace American Order* (New York: Oxford University Press, 2021).

86. "Most Americans Have 'Cold' Views of China. Here's What They Think About China, in Their Own Words," Pew Research Center, June 30, 2021, www.pewresearch.org/global/2021/06/30/most-americans-have-cold -views-of-china-heres-what-they-think-about-china-in-their-own-words.

87. "Most Americans Have 'Cold' Views of China," Pew Research Center.

88. Melanie Hart and Blaine Johnson, "Mapping China's Global Governance Ambitions," Center for American Progress, February 28, 2019, www.americanprogress.org/issues/security/reports/2019/02/28/466768 /mapping-chinas-global-governance-ambitions.

89. Stenslie and Galtung, *49 Myths*.

# 7

# Is Xi a
# New Mao?

On July 1, 2021, Xi Jinping celebrated the centenary of China's Communist Party. To mark this highly symbolic occasion, 70,000 Chinese perfectly choreographed by the party apparatus, each waving a five-star red flag, assembled in Tiananmen Square in the heart of Beijing. Xi waved from the podium of the Gate of Heavenly Peace, the main entrance to the Forbidden City, the same place where Mao Zedong had proclaimed the People's Republic of China on October 1, 1949. Xi wore a grey Mao suit, while the other leaders wore Western suits. Under the feet of the party leader hung a huge portrait of Mao Zedong, in a grey suit identical to the one worn by Xi. At the end of the ceremony, Xi raised his right arm, a gesture precisely the same as that made by the millions of Mao statues to be found everywhere in China. For those present, it must have been clear beyond all doubt that Mao and Xi were cut from the same cloth.

Long before this anniversary party in Beijing, many China observers claimed that Xi had ambitions to be a new Mao Zedong. One of these, Elizabeth C. Economy, researcher at the Council on Foreign Relations in New York, said, "Like Mao, Xi has prioritized strengthening the party, inculcating collective socialist values, and, rooting out nonbelievers. Like Mao, who invoked 'domestic and foreign reactionaries' to build nationalist sentiment and solidify the party's legitimacy, Xi has adopted a consistent refrain of unspecified but 'ubiquitous' internal and external threats. And like Mao, Xi has encouraged the creation of a cult of personality around himself."[1]

It is easy to point out the resemblances between Mao and Xi when it comes to personal charisma, dominant role in the party, and hard line on political and other opponents in China.[2] Without doubt the Xi cult is a blast from the Mao past and a sign that Xi wants to be the new "red emperor," a despotic lifelong ruler just like Mao.[3] Since Xi remained in power after the twentieth party congress in October 2022, even more will draw parallels between the two party leaders, who claim to be the mightiest in the history of the People's Republic of China.

Is Xi a new Mao?

## The Limits of Parallels

Tony C. Lee, China researcher at Freie Universität Berlin, has analyzed the two Chinese leaders by applying the five-factor, or Big Five, model of personality to find out if Xi is a new Mao. This model is based on the idea that an individual's personality can be understood with the aid of five overall factors: extroversion, agreeableness, conscientiousness, neuroticism, and openness to experience. Lee reckons Mao and Xi score about the same on openness to experience and extroversion but differently on conscientiousness, agreeableness, and neuroticism. Mao and Xi can be described as charismatic leaders as both score high on extroversion—that is the extent to which people get energy from, seek out, and enjoy social events and are able to assert themselves. But Mao has lower tolerance of political opponents, scoring high on neuroticism and low on agreeableness, while Xi has a greater need to perform, scoring high on conscientiousness. "Conscientious" describes a person who is organized, systematic, punctual, achievement oriented, and dependable.[4]

Such comparisons based on personality psychology make captivating reading but, in our opinion, are of limited use for understanding how China is developing. Psychologizing at distance of a leader embalmed in a mausoleum in Beijing and one behind the walls of Zhongnanhai in the same city is a difficult, perhaps impossible exercise.

One can also question the value of comparing these two leaders since more than sixty years separate their governments. China now is nowhere near the same as China then. In 1949 when Mao took over, about 500 million destitute, mostly rural Chinese were traumatized by national chaos after the collapse of the empire, foreign occupation, and civil war. China's share of the global economy was scarcely 3.8 percent, life expectancy was barely forty years, approximately 80 percent of the population were illiterate, and only 20,000 graduated annually from institutions of higher education. The country's armed forces were a ragged militia. And the world was entering the Cold War.

In 2012 Xi came to power in a country about to enter the world stage as a superpower. It had a population of 1.4 billion, mostly urban, full of optimism and belief in a bright future. The country's share of the global economy had grown to more than 15 percent and was expected to become the world's biggest in the next few years. Life expectancy had doubled to almost eighty years, 7 million young Chinese graduated yearly from institutions of higher education, and Chinese citizens could travel and realize themselves. A world-class military power, China was racing at full speed into a bilateral global order dominated by the United States and itself.[5] Mao belonged to an analog era and ruled over a people isolated from the world, while Xi lives in a digital era and rules over a highly globalized population. While Mao's word was law and he could manipulate and mobilize the masses to achieve his political will, Xi has to relate to a far more interwoven and enlightened public.

## Good Ruler, Bad Ruler

Those who point out the similarities between Mao and Xi do so mainly to warn of the dangers of developments under the latter's rule. Mao is brought forward as a horrifying example of how wrong it can go when a despot is at the helm. Francis Fukuyama, who has studied political developments in China, points out that the traditional Chinese authoritarian system had a weakness known as the "bad ruler" phenomenon. A dictator with few if any limits on his executive power, such as independent courts, free media, or an elected legislature, can do fantastic things when the ruler is good. Correspondingly, a bad ruler can inflict on the state and the people irreparable damage because there are no limitations on his power. And there have been many bad rulers in China's history. This is a problem the Chinese have not yet solved, according to the American political scientist. Fukuyama thinks Mao, who with the Great Leap Forward and the Cultural Revolution brought unimaginable tragedies on his people, was the last in the line of bad rulers. Even if, as the Chinese Communist Party claims, Mao was 70 percent right and 30 percent wrong, that 30 percent exacted a steep price.[6]

So what about Xi Jinping? Is he a good or bad ruler? "Xi is a good ruler. Let us keep him as long as we can," claimed a Chinese academic in Hong Kong.[7] Those interested in historic long lines might add that of the 422 rulers who have governed China, only a few have been enlightened and competent. Without doubt Xi has a strong feeling of ownership and responsibility for the country. He is aware that the party and China face a series of existential challenges and clearly regards himself as the best suited of the 1.4 billion Chinese to tackle them. Xi's dream is not empty rhetoric for there is reason to believe that he genuinely believes it himself.

"To realize his China Dream he needs power and time. If Xi remains in office for longer than his two terms he will get more time and no new ruler will be able to overturn his decisions," commented the same Hong Kong–based academic.[8] He is only one inhabitant in the word's most highly populated country. But China has for years ranked number one in global government trust rankings. According to the "2022 Edelman Trust Barometer"—Edelman is the world's biggest public relations consulting firm—Chinese trust in their government reached 91 percent in 2021, up 9 percent from the previous year.[9] A poll conducted by the Ash Center for more than fifteen years finds that more than 90 percent of the Chinese people year after year remain happy with their own government.[10] Another poll published by the *Washington Post* in July 2020 showed that as many as 98 percent of the Chinese trusted their government.[11] All polls showed, however, that local authorities scored significantly lower on the trust rankings than the central government in Beijing. The trust the Chinese central government enjoys from the people is sky high compared to the confidence most Western leaders enjoy among their own populations.[12] How has the Chinese government under the leadership of the Communist Party won the high trust of the people? While Xi Jinping's international reputation took a dive because of Covid-19, other surveys showed that at home his reputation rose because of the way he tackled the pandemic.[13] China was the only major economy to have grown during the pandemic. Other sources of Xi's popularity are probably his focus on economic redistribution and the harsh anticorruption campaign. Of course, one should take all political opinion surveys in China with a pinch of salt. Nonetheless, in sum, they indicate considerable popular support for Xi.

Obviously, at the same time many Chinese experience Xi Jinping as a bad ruler. In Xi's China, few dare criticize the nation's head for fear of reprisal. The fate of Nobel Peace Prize winner Liu Xiaobo, who died in prison, was a clear warning. Still, it is reasonable to suppose that segments of the population are far from content with the way things have gone over the past decade. Liberal intellectuals, academics, publishers, and journalists with a different vision for China than his dream are scared into silence. No other country is arresting more journalists than Xi's China.[14]

Activists fighting to keep what remains of a civil society and whistle-blowers who try to put the spotlight on blameworthy conditions in the land have been gagged. Among them we can mention journalist Zhang Zhan and doctor Li Wenliang. In autumn 2019 they both gave early warnings that the virus was spreading in Wuhan. Zhang Zhan is now serving a four-year prison sentence, while Li Wenliang has died from Covid. In Hong Kong, the democracy movement has been crushed, a powerful signal to any Mainlanders with democratic ideas in their heads. In Xi's China, ethnic minorities such as Uighurs, Tibetans, and Mongols experience pressure from state-sponsored Han nationalism. Faith communities—Muslims, Christians, and Buddhists—are persecuted all over the country. There is little reason to think Xi is popular with these persecuted groups. Even if it is probable that Xi has the support of the political elite for his centralization of power and disciplining of the cadres, deep down many likely think that the rehabilitation of Mao is too extreme and that the personality cult, the anticorruption campaign, Han nationalism, and the assertive foreign policy have all gone too far.

## Master Lu's Warning

Regardless of whether Xi is a good or bad ruler, the Mao era should serve as a warning of the considerable risk of so much power in one person's hands. It is not without reason that Deng laid down the principle of collective leadership and introduced the two-term limit on how long a leader could stay in office.

There will be an increasing risk of misjudgments and poor decisions with a self-willed Xi at the wheel. Even if it is hard to know how decisions are made, one might think collective leadership would make it possible to air different opinions and that decisions would be made after reaching a consensus. Obviously, such processes can be slow, and sometimes decisions are not made fast enough.

However, collective leadership could act as an important risk-management mechanism. Openness to different perspectives helps ensure that impractical or dangerous ideas are rejected, and one can hardly claim that the party made disastrous mistakes under Xi's two predecessors, Jiang Zemin and Hu Jintao. Under Xi, the collective has been replaced by one-man rule. Expressing opinions that contradict that one man has been criminalized. The crime, called "reckless talk about the party's center" (妄议中央) in paragraph 46 of the party's disciplinary rules, is punishable by exclusion from the party.[15]

Xi has launched many new initiatives simultaneously. Things move fast. Even for a workaholic such as Xi, there are limits to how much information he can absorb and how many issues he can master. There is considerable danger of misjudgment and bad decisions if Xi is to make all the calls, not listen to advice, and surround himself with "yes men." Critical voices in Beijing have long whispered that Xi's inner circle exclusively consists of those he relies on and that these are not necessarily those most suited.[16] He only promotes servile yes men—those who will never correct him and who only bring him good news. This became very clear during the twentieth party congress, where the new Politburo and its Standing Committee were made up exclusively of Xi loyalists. It is striking that none of Xi's six colleagues in the Standing Committee have their own family connections or a strong regional or factional power base. They all have a common background. In this respect, they constitute what Victor Shih refers to as "coalitions of the weak," with which strong leaders such as Mao and Xi prefer to surround themselves in order to reduce the risk of political opposition.[17] Without their own power base, these men are at the mercy of Xi, and their positions and influence rest entirely on his retaining power. The potentially disastrous consequences of authoritarian rulers being surrounded by yes men are clearly demonstrated by Vladimir Putin's miscalculated war in Ukraine.

The warning Master Lu uttered more than two thousand years ago is still appropriate today: "No less than three hundred astrologers sit staring at the stars. But these good men, frightened as they are of insulting the emperor, dare not tell him the truth or point out his mistakes."[18] In other words, this is a form of government that has plagued China through the imperial era until today. As he stays on in power, will Xi bring as great disasters on the Chinese people as Mao? Impossible to say. We must hope not. But since China's military power and ambitions both regionally and globally are growing, grave dangers of misjudgment threaten world peace. Taiwan is a throbbing boil for Beijing. Several times Xi has threatened to take the island by force, so an attack in the not-too-distant future is not unthinkable.[19] Recent visits by US Congresswoman Nancy Pelosi and other US politicians to the island and promises of American support resulted in Beijing holding huge naval exercises all around the island, and Chinese fighter planes are regularly violating Taiwan's airspace. As Putin's military invasion of Ukraine clearly illustrates, the outcome of any war is highly uncertain. War could end in disaster also for China—and East Asia and the rest of the world.

Furthermore, with such a dominant leader as Xi, the party risks losing some of its anchorage. As mentioned earlier, formerly certain rules and practices stabilized the political system—there was a certain power balance among the top leaders through representation in certain key posts, the protection of the interests of individual members of the elite (e.g., the immunity of members of the Politburo from prosecution), compulsory retirement, and term limits. These elite norms had wide backing. However, in his first decade Xi has scrapped them all. In doing so, he may have removed part of the foundation of the regime's stability.

Such norms have been a strength for the regime since they made possible an orderly change of leadership. The most orderly change in the People's Republic's history ironically took place in 2012, when Xi came to power and, unlike his predecessors, immediately gained all three of the most important posts. Change of leadership is the Achilles' heel of any authoritarian regime. History is full of examples of regimes that have collapsed because of elite conflicts linked to the change of leadership. The orderly system China has had over the past decades is unique in the world of Communist dictatorships, where leaders usually sit for life. Leader circulation has given the Chinese system a vital adjustment mechanism. When new leaders have come to power, they have been able to a correct the political course of their predecessors and therefore, at last to some extent, satisfy the wishes and demands of the population. Unlike his predecessors, Xi has not groomed a successor. The members of the Politburo's Standing Committee are all in their sixties and, with the possible exception of Ding Xuexiang, too old to be the next general secretary. Xi himself was fifty-four years old when, as an aspiring leader, he was promoted to the Standing Committee. As Xi seems determined to stay in power indefinitely, this is a breach of the established practice of leadership circulation and undermines the obvious advantages this has had for political stability.

The consequence of a strong Xi Jinping might therefore be a weaker party. Besides, Xi has got so much power he can hardly relinquish it, even if he should want to. A Chinese proverb says, "When riding a tiger it is difficult to dismount" (骑虎难下)—because then he will be eaten.[20] During his first decade in power, Xi has indubitably accumulated many enemies. These will throw themselves on him once he is no longer in power. The longer he sits, the more bitter his enemies will become, and discontent in the system and in the population will increase. It is typical for dictators to paint themselves into a corner.

Younger, aspiring leaders can no longer sit patiently and wait their turn. They will conspire against the ruler to take his place.

Simultaneously, everything that goes wrong will be blamed on him. As with Mao, there is a danger that Xi will become more and more paranoid and crueler and crueler. Xi has broken the norm of indemnity to prosecution that previous top leaders enjoyed. Because he treated cadres so mercilessly during his anticorruption campaign, once he leaves office, he and his family will be in grave danger. Statistics make grim reading for Xi: political scientists Alexandre Debs and H. E. Goemans have calculated that 41 percent of authoritarian rulers either end up in jail or in exile or die within a year of falling from power, compared to 7 percent of democratically elected leaders.[21] Out of fear for his own security and the life and health of his family and allies, Xi will probably hang on to power at any price.

As we wrote earlier, Mao was very preoccupied with the fate of Chinese emperors to try to avoid the errors that led to their fall. One important lesson was that an elite coup was the most likely cause of a dynasty's fall. Most dynasties were overturned not by invading nomad hordes or peasant risings but by elite groups that were part of the established regime. The elite understand how the system works, have access to resources and weapons, and know the way to the emperor's bedroom.[22] We find the same pattern outside China and also in modern times. Political scientist Milan W. Svolvik has found that two of three authoritarian leaders from 1948 to 2008 were toppled by their own elites.[23] Xi, who like Mao has read a lot of Chinese history, knows that he has most reason to fear other party tops, especially if they conspire with the security and armed forces.

At the time of writing, a coup seems unlikely. The elite's collective interest in keeping the Communist Party in power seems intact, something that will dampen any desire to challenge Xi, particularly given the direct bond that has been tied between his leadership and the party's fate over the past ten years. At the same time, the threshold for conspiring against the leader has become very high. Far more than ever is at stake now that China has been unleashed as a superpower. Moreover, Xi controls the other leaders, where they live, travel, and meet. New technology gives Xi the possibility of surveilling their telephones and email and accessing all kinds of compromising material. But all this may not be enough to hinder future elite conflicts.

While the impact of such conflicts was once restricted to China, destabilization of the regime would now shake the whole world.

## Conclusion

Is Xi Jinping here to stay? This is the $64,000 question that preoccupies any China Hand in the wake of the twentieth party congress. There are as many answers as there are diplomats, researchers, journalists, and other interested in this question. In a conversation between a China observer and a supposedly well-placed party member in Beijing, the latter answered in this way:

> CHINA OBSERVER: Will Xi rule after the next party congress [in 2022]?
> PARTY MEMBER: Yes, certainly.
> CHINA OBSERVER: What about the one after that [in 2027]?
> PARTY MEMBER: Probably.
> CHINA OBSERVER: But what about the one after that [in 2032]?
> PARTY MEMBER: No, then we'll tell him he is too old.[24]

This is as good an answer as any. No China observer has the answer; nor do we. Xi seems to be a healthy and fit sixty-nine-year-old who can lead the Communist Party for ten or twenty more years, should he wish to. But as we have pointed out many times, Xi is good at hiding his intentions. No one outside Zhongnanhai can say with certainty how long Xi intends to rule China or what strategies he might use to achieve that end. As we have shown, much is unclear about how he came to power ten years ago. The extent of any backing of the political elite for his centralization of power, his anticorruption campaign, and his tightening of party discipline is still an open question. How much support he has among the Chinese people—whether he is regarded as a good or bad ruler—remains unknown, despite the efforts of statisticians and social scientists. In other words, the most central questions about Xi's China are shrouded in mystery. The lack of credible, documented information in an ocean of speculation, combined with a tendency among

China observers to see the country through Western, normative spectacles, makes understanding China challenging.

Nonetheless, it is more important than ever to acquire knowledge about the country. The past decade has shown with all clarity how dominant a political actor Xi is. China's leader is good at hiding his intentions. This in itself fires up rumors and speculation about what happens in Beijing's corridors of power. We have tried to avoid speculation and wishful thinking. Instead, we have put the spotlight on Xi's background and what he has done and said in his first decade in power. This is the key to understanding the new superpower.

## Notes

1. Elizabeth C. Economy, "China's Neo-Maoist Moment," *Foreign Affairs*, October 1, 2019.

2. See, for example, Jack Erickson, "Is Xi Jinping the New Mao Zedong?" *National Interest*, November 2, 2020; Doug Bandow, "Xi Jinping Wants to Become the New Mao," Cato Institute, May 26, 2020, www.cato.org/commentary/xi-jinping-wants-become-new-mao.

3. "Beware the Cult of Xi," *The Economist*, March 2, 2016; Hannah Beech, "China's Chairman Builds a Cult of Personality," *Time Magazine*, March 31, 2016.

4. Tony C. Lee, "Can Xi Jinping Be the Next Mao Zedong? Using the Big Five Model to Study Political Leadership," *Journal of Chinese Political Science* 23, no. 4 (2018): 473–497.

5. For some interesting figures on macroeconomic and social development in China, see "The People's Republic of China: 70 Years of Changes," *South China Morning Post*, October 1, 2019, https://multimedia.scmp.com/info graphics/news/china/article/3030959/china-70th-anniversary/index.html.

6. Francis Fukuyama, "China Has Banished Bo but Not the 'Bad Emperor' Problem," *Financial Times*, May 10, 2012.

7. Conversations in Hong Kong, October 2018.

8. Conversations in Hong Kong, October 2018.

9. "2022 Edelman Trust Barometer," Edelman, September 2022, www.edelman.com/trust/2022-trust-barometer.

10. Dan Harsha, "Taking China's Pulse," *Harvard Gazette*, July 9, 2020.

11. Cary Wu, "Did the Pandemic Shake Chinese Citizens' Trust in Their Government? We Surveyed Nearly 20,000 People to Find Out," *Washington Post*, May 5, 2020.

12. "2022 Edelman Trust Barometer," Edelman, September 2022.

13. "Unfavourable Views of China Reach Historic Highs in Many Countries," Pew Research Center, October 6, 2020; "2022 Edelman Trust Barometer," Edelman, September 2022; Cary Wu, "How Chinese Citizens View Their Government's Coronavirus Response," *The Conversation*, June 4, 2020.

14. Niall McCarthy, "Where the Most Journalists Are Imprisoned Worldwide," Statista, January 4, 2021.

15. Victor Shih, *Coalitions of the Weak: Elite Politics in China from Mao's Stratagem to the Rise of Xi* (Cambridge: Cambridge University Press, 2022).

16. Conversations in Hong Kong, November 2018, and, Paris, June 2019.

17. "The Chinese Communist Party Disciplinary Regulations," China Law Translate, October 22, 2015, www.chinalawtranslate.com. See also "We're Not Having This Discussion," China Media Project, October 22, 2015, https://medium.com/china-media-project/we-re-not-having-this-discussion-fe6668495add.

18. Quoted in Torbjørn Færøyvik, "Formannen for alt" [Chairman of everything], *Dagbladet*, August 16, 2021, www.dagbladet.no/meninger/formannen-for-alt/74102558.

19. See, for example, Yew Lun Tian and Yimou Lee, "China's Xi Pledges 'Reunification' with Taiwan, Gets Stern Rebuke," Reuters, July 1, 2021.

20. Halvor Eifring in the podcast *De mektige* [The mighty].

21. Alexandra Debs and H. E. Goemans, "Regime Type, the Fate of Leaders, and War," *American Political Science Review* 104, no. 3 (August 2010): 430–445, https://cpb-us-w2.wpmucdn.com/campuspress.yale.edu/dist/7/2534/files/2019/07/Debs-Goemans-2010-Regime-Type-the-Fate-of-Leaders-and-War.pdf.

22. Wang, "Can the Chinese Communist Party Learn from Chinese Emperors?" 62.

23. Milan Svolik, *The Politics of Authoritarian Rule* (Cambridge: Cambridge University Press, 2012), 14, 85–100.

24. Conversation quoted by Joseph Torigian in Smith and Lim, "Xi Dada and Daddy."

# Appendix 1

## Timeline of the People's Republic of China

| | |
|---|---|
| 1949 | Foundation of the People's Republic of China. |
| 1958–1961 | Mao Zedong's Great Leap Forward campaign. |
| 1966–1976 | The Cultural Revolution. |
| 1976 | Death of Mao. |
| 1978 | Deng Xiaoping ascends to power. |
| 1978 | Deng initiates "reform and opening." |
| 1982 | Deng sets term limits for top party leaders. |
| 1986 | China opens its economy to foreign investments. |
| 1989 | Democratic uprising crushed at Tiananmen Square. |
| 1989 | Jiang Zemin becomes general secretary of the Chinese Communist Party (CCP). |
| 1992 | China becomes the world's third-biggest economy (after Japan and the United States). |
| 2002 | Hu Jintao becomes general secretary of the CCP. |
| 2008 | Beijing hosts the Summer Olympic Games. |
| 2010 | China becomes the second-biggest world economy (after the United States). |
| 2012 | Xi Jinping becomes general secretary of the CCP. |
| 2018 | Term limits on the presidency in China are abolished. |

| | |
|---|---|
| 2019 | Novel coronavirus (Covid-19) outbreak in Wuhan, Hubei Province. |
| 2021 | China's Communist Party celebrates its centenary. |
| 2022 | Xi Jinping wins unprecedented third term as general secretary. |

# Appendix 2

## Timeline of Xi Jinping's Life and Career

| | |
|---|---|
| 1953 | Born on June 15 in Beijing. |
| 1969–1975 | So-called reeducation (i.e., forced labor in the countryside). |
| 1974 | Member of the Chinese Communist Party (CCP). |
| 1975–1979 | Chemical engineering student at Tsinghua University, Beijing. |
| 1979–1982 | Secretary for defense minister Geng Biao. |
| 1982–1985 | Various party posts in Hebei Province. |
| 1985–1995 | Deputy mayor in Xiamen, Fujian Province. |
| 1987 | Marriage to Peng Liyuan. |
| 1995–1999 | Vice party secretary in Fujian. |
| 1999–2022 | Governor of Fujian. |
| 2002–2007 | Governor and party secretary in Zhejiang Province. |
| 2007 | Party secretary in Shanghai. |
| 2007 | Promotion to membership of the Politburo's Standing Committee of the CCP. |
| 2008 | Election as vice president. |
| 2012 | Promotion to general secretary of the CCP. |
| 2013 | Election as president. |

| | |
|---|---|
| 2017 | Second term as general secretary of the CCP. |
| 2017 | *Xi's Thoughts* made part of the party's constitution. |
| 2018 | Term limits on leadership posts abolished. |
| 2018 | Second term as president. |
| 2022 | Third term as general secretary of the CCP. |
| 2023 | Third term as president. |

# Selected Bibliography

Allison, Graham. "The Chairman of Everything: Why Chinese President Xi Jinping Will Change History." *New Statesman*. December 4, 2017. www.belfercenter.org/publication/chairman-everything-why-chinese -president-xi-jinping-will-change-history.

Andrésy, Agnès. *Xi Jinping: Red China, the Next Generation*. Lanham, MD: University Press of America, 2016.

Anonymous. *Liangjiahe Village: A Story of Chinese President Xi Jinping*. Xian: Shaanxi People's Publishing House Co. Ltd, 2018.

Apor, Balázs, Jan C. Behrends, Polly Jones, and E. A. Rees (eds.). *The Leader Cult in Communist Dictatorships*. London: Palgrave Macmillan, 2004.

"習近平南巡後" [After Xi Jinping's southern tour]. *Apple Daily*.

Aust, Stefan, and Adrian Geiges. *Xi Jinping: The Most Powerful Man in the World*. Cambridge, UK: Polity, 2022.

Bandow, Doug. "Xi Jinping Wants to Become the New Mao." Cato Institute. May 26, 2020. www.cato.org/commentary/xi-jinping-wants-become-new -mao.

Bandurski, David. "Tracing the 'People's Leader.'" China Media Project. January 21, 2020. https://chinamediaproject.org/2020/01/21/tracing-the -peoples-leader.

Barmé, Geremie R. "Tyger, Tyger—a Fearful Symmetry." *China Story Journal*. October 16, 2014. https://archive.thechinastory.org/2014/10/tyger-tyger -a-fearful-symmetry.

Blanchette, Jude. "Xi's Gamble." *Foreign Affairs*. July/August 2021. www .foreignaffairs.com/articles/china/2021-06-22/xis-gamble.

Blanchette, Jude D. *China's New Red Guards. The Return of Radicalism and the Rebirth of Mao Zedong*. New York: Oxford University Press, 2019.

Bo Zhiyue. "Chinas Fifth-Generation Leaders: Characteristics of the New Elite and Pathways to Leadership." In Robert S. Ross and Jo Inge Bekkevold (eds.). *China in the Era of Xi Jinping: Domestic and Foreign Policy Challenges*. Washington DC: Georgetown University Press, 2016.

Bo Zhiyue. "In China, an Ode to 'Grandpa Xi.'" *The Diplomat*. June 17, 2015.

Bostock, Bill. "Xi Jinping Could Revive Mao Zedong's Long-Dormant Title of 'Chairman' to Help Him Maintain Total Control, Experts Say." *Business Insider*. August 26, 2020.

Bougon, François. *Inside the Mind of Xi Jinping*. London: C. Hurst & Co. Ltd., 2018.

Bourdieu, Pierre. "The Forms of Capital." In John G. Richardson (ed.). *Handbook of Theory and Research for the Sociology of Education*. New York: Greenwood Press, 1986.

Bourdieu, Pierre. *Language and Symbolic Power*. Cambridge, MA: Harvard University Press, 1991.

Branovitch, Nimrod. "A Strong Leader for a Time of Crisis: Xi Jinping's Strongman Politics as a Collective Response to Regime Weakness." *Journal of Contemporary China* 30, no. 128 (2021): 249–265.

Brown, Kerry. *CEO, China: The Rise of Xi Jinping*. London: I. B. Tauris, 2016.

Brown, Kerry (ed.), *China and the EU in Context*. London: Palgrave MacMillan, 2014.

Brown, Kerry. "Xi Jinping's Leadership Style: Master or Servant?" *Asian International Studies Review* 17, no. 2 (December 2016): 143–158.

Brown, Kerry. "Xi's China and Han Fei: A Lesson in Authority." *open Democracy*. December 18, 2015. www.opendemocracy.net/en/han-feis-china-shiver-of-authority.

Brown, Kerry. *The World According to Xi: Everything You Need to Know About the New China*. London: I. B. Taurus, 2018.

Bruce, Dickson. *The Dictator's Dilemma: The Chinese Communist Party's Strategy for Survival*. New York: Oxford University Press, 2016.

Bueno de Mesquita, Bruce. *The Dictator's Handbook: Why Bad Behavior Is Almost Always Good Politics*. New York: PublicAffairs, 2012.

Cabestan, Jean-Pierre. "Is Xi Jinping the Reformist Leader China Needs?" *China Perspectives*. October 2012. https://journals.openedition.org/chinaperspectives/5969.

Cabestan, Jean-Pierre. "Political Changes in China Since the 19th CCP Congress: Xi Jinping Is Not Weaker but More Contested." *East Asia* 36 (2019): 1–21. https://link.springer.com/article/10.1007/s12140-019-09305-x.

Carothers, Christopher. "Xi's Anti-corruption Campaign: An All-Purpose Governing Tool." *China Leadership Monitor*. March 1, 2021. www.prcleader .org/carothers.

Carrico, Kevin Joseph. *The Great Han Race, Nationalism, and Tradition in China Today*. Oakland: University of California Press, 2017.

"Chairman of Everything." *The Economist*. April 2, 2016.

Chan Ying-Kit and Fei Chen (eds). *Alternative Representations of the Past: The Politics of History in Modern China*. Berlin and Boston: De Gruyter Oldenbourg, 2020.

Chan, Alfred. *Xi Jinping: Political Career, Governance, and Leadership, 1953–2018*. Oxford: Oxford University Press, 2022.

Chan, Minnie. "Xi Jinping Sharpened His Political Skills in Fujian." *South China Morning Post*. October 2, 2012.

Chen Weiss, Jessica. "How Hawkish Is the Chinese Public? Another Look at 'Rising Nationalism' and Chinese Foreign Policy." *Journal of Contemporary China*. 28, no. 119 (2019).

Cheng, Dean. "China's Xi Jinping's New Hard Line and the U.S.-Japan Alliance." Heritage Foundation. February 12, 2013. www.heritage.org /node/11958/print-display.

Cheng Li. *Chinese Politics in the Xi Jinping Era: Reassessing Collective Leadership*. Washington, DC: Brookings Institution Press, 2016.

Cheng Li. "The End of CCP's Resilient Authoritarianism? A Tripartite Assessment of Shifting Power in China." *China Quarterly* 211 (2012): 595–623.

Cheng Li. "Xi Jinping's Inner Circle (Parts 1–5)." *China Leadership Monitor*. 2014–2015. www.brookings.edu/wp-content/uploads/2016/06/Xi-Jinping -Inner-Circle.pdf.

Cheng Li and Eve Cary. "The Last Year of Hu's Leadership: Hu's to Blame?" Jamestown Foundation. December 20, 2011.

Choi Chi-yuk and Josephine Ma. "Zhou Yongkang, Bo Xilai Among Elite Prisoners in China's 'Tigers' Cage' Qincheng Growing Vegetables and Wearing Suits." *South China Morning Post*. January 13, 2019.

Chongyang Institute for Financial Studies. "疫后中国将领导世界？时殷弘：相反，中国应战略收缩" [Should China lead the world after the pandemic?].

Chu, Margaret. "A Catholic Voice Out of Communist China." Mindszenty. November 1998. www.mindszenty.org/report/1998/nov98/mr_nov98.html.

CIA. *Intelligence Report: The Cultural Revolution and the Ninth Party Congress*. CIA. October 1, 1969.

Clarke, Michael. "China's Hidden Totalitarianism." *National Interest*. August 29, 2018.

Dai Xu. "2020对美国的4个想不到与10个新认识" [Four unexpected things and ten new understandings about the USA in 2020]. *Guancha*. July 8, 2020. https://user.guancha.cn/main/content?id=342787.

Debs, Alexandra, and H. E. Goemans. "Regime Type, the Fate of Leaders, and War." *American Political Science Review* 104, no. 3 (August 2010): 430–445. https://cpb-us-w2.wpmucdn.com/campuspress.yale.edu/dist/7/2534/files/2019/07/Debs-Goemans-2010-Regime-Type-the-Fate-of-Leaders-and-War.pdf.

Deng Xiaoping. "Peace and Development Are the Two Outstanding Issues in the World Today." Selected Works of Deng Xiaoping, March 4, 1985. https://dengxiaopingworks.wordpress.com/2013/03/18/peace-and-development-are-the-two-outstanding-issues-in-the-world-today.

Deng Yanhua and Yang Guobin, "Pollution and Protest in China: Environmental Mobilization in Context." *China Quarterly* 214 (2013).

Dikötter, Frank. *Mao's Great Famine: The History of China's Most Devastating Catastrophe, 1958–62*. New York: Walker & Company, 2010.

Ding, Arthur S., and Jagannath P. Panda (eds.). *Chinese Politics and Foreign Policy Under Xi Jinping*. New York: Routledge, 2021.

Doshi, Rush. *The Long Game: China's Grand Strategy to Displace American Order*. New York: Oxford University Press, 2021.

Economy, Elizabeth C. "China's Neo-Maoist Moment." *Foreign Affairs*. October 1, 2019.

Economy, Elizabeth C. *The Third Revolution: Xi Jinping and the New Chinese State*. New York: Oxford University Press, 2018.

Erickson, Jack. "Is Xi Jinping the New Mao Zedong?" *National Interest*. November 2, 2020.

Fenby, Jonathan. *The Penguin History of Modern China: The Fall and Rise of a Great Power, 1850–2008*. London: Allen Lane, 2008.

Fewsmith, Joseph. *Rethinking Chinese Politics*. Cambridge: Cambridge University Press, 2021.

Fewsmith, Joseph. "The Sixteenth National Party Congress: The Succession That Didn't Happen." *China Quarterly* 173 (2003): 1–16.

Fewsmith, Joseph, and Andrew J. Nathan. "Authoritarian Resilience Revisited." *Journal of Contemporary China*. September 23, 2018.

Fong, Victor K. "Imagining the Future from History: The Tang Dynasty and the 'China Dream.'" In Ying-Kit Chan and Fei Chen (eds.). *Alternative Representations of the Past: The Politics of History in Modern China*. Berlin and Boston: De Gruyter Oldenbourg, 2020.

Forsby, Andreas B. "What Is Behind China's Diplomacy of Indignation?" *The Diplomat*. November 13, 2020.

Fukuyama, Francis. "China Has Banished Bo but Not the 'Bad Emperor' Problem." *Financial Times*. May 10, 2012. www.ft.com/content/c71ff938-99c9-11e1-aa6d-00144feabdc0.

Gan, Nectar. "President Xi Jinping's Corruption Crackdown Linked to Officials' Suicides." *South China Morning Post*. May 3, 2015.

Gan, Nectar. "Want to Escape Poverty? Replace Pictures of Jesus with Xi Jinping, Christian Villagers Urged." *South China Morning Post*. November 14, 2017.

Ganault, John. *The Rise and Fall of the House of Bo*. Melbourne: Penguin Random House, Australia, 2012.

Ghosh, Iman. "How China Overtook the U.S. as the World's Major Trading Partner." *Visual Capitalist*. January 22, 2020.

Glassman, Ronald. "Legitimacy and Manufactured Charisma." *Social Research* 42, no. 4 (1975): 615–636.

Goodman, David S. G. (ed.). *Handbook of Politics of China*. Cheltenham, UK: Edward Elgar, 2015.

Gries, Peter Hays, Derek Steiger, and Tao Wang. "Popular Nationalism and China's Japan Policy: The Diaoyu Islands Protests, 2012–2013." *Journal of Contemporary China* 25, no. 98 (2016).

Grønmo, Sigmund, Ann Nilsen, and Karen Christensen (eds). *Ulikhet: Sosiologiske perspektiver og analyser* [Inequality: sociological perspectives and analyses]. Bergen: Fagbokforlaget, 2021.

Hart, Brian. "Creating the Cult of Xi Jinping: The Chinese Dream as a Leader Symbol." *Cornell International Affairs Review* 9 (2016).

Hart, Melanie, and Blaine Johnson. "Mapping China's Global Governance Ambitions." Center for American Progress. February 28, 2019. www.americanprogress.org/issues/security/reports/2019/02/28/466768/mapping-chinas-global-governance-ambitions.

Horsley, Jamie P. "Party Leadership and Rule of Law in the Xi Jinping Era: What Does an Ascendant Chinese Communist Party Mean for China's Legal Development?" Brookings. September 2019. https://law.yale.edu/sites/default/files/area/center/china/document/horsley_china_party-_legal_development.pdf.

Howell, Jude, and Jane Duckett, "Reassessing the Hu-Wen Era: A Golden Age or Lost Decade for Social Policy in China?" *China Quarterly* 237 (2018): 1–14.

Inoguchi, Takashi, G. John Ikenberry, and Yoichiro Sato (eds.). *The U.S.-Japan Security Alliance: Regional Multilateralism*. New York: Palgrave Macmillan, 2011.

Ji Xianlin. *The Cowshed: Memories of the Cultural Revolution*. New York: New York Review Books, 1998.

Kissinger, Henry. *Does America Need a Foreign Policy? Toward a Diplomacy for the 21st Century*. New York: Simon & Schuster, 2001.

Koesel, Karrie J. "Legitimacy, Resilience, and Political Education in Russia and China: Learning to Be Loyal." In Karrie J. Koesel, Valerie J. Bunce, and Jessica Chen Weiss (eds.). *Citizens and the State in Authoritarian Regimes: Comparing China and Russia*. New York: Oxford University Press, 2020.

Koesel, Karrie J., Valerie J. Bunce, and Jessica Chen Weiss (eds). *Citizens and the State in Authoritarian Regimes: Comparing China and Russia.* New York: Oxford University Press, 2020.

Lam, Willy Wo-Lap. *Chinese Politics in the Era of Xi Jinping: Renaissance, Reform, or Retrogression?* New York: Routledge, 2015.

Lee, Tony C. "Can Xi Jinping Be the Next Mao Zedong? Using the Big Five Model to Study Political Leadership." *Journal of Chinese Political Science* 23, no. 4 (2018): 473–497.

Liu, Melinda. "Is China's New U.S. Ambassador a 'Wolf Warrior'—or a Fox?" *Foreign Policy.* August 10, 2021.

Liu Yazhou. "照耀中国梦的思想火炬" [An ideological torch shining on the Chinese dream]. *Renmin ribao.* February 4, 2015. http://politics.people.com.cn/n/2015/0204/c1001-26502540.html.

Lungu, Andrei. "China's Next President: Reading the Tea Leaves of Chinese Politics." *The Diplomat.* September 29, 2017.

Lynch, Tyler. "China Has Brought Forth a Xi Dada: How China Is Making and Breaking the Personality Cult of Xi Jinping." *Undergraduate Journal of Politics, Policy and Society* 3, no. 1 (2020): 77–89. www.ujpps.com/index.php/ujpps/article/view/71.

Ma Haoliang. "90多年产生约70名常委 命运各异" [The seventy members of the Politburo's Standing Committee over ninety years—different fates]. *Dagong Bao.* March 2, 2015. http://news.takungpao.com/special/szqh_changwei.

MacFarquhar, Roderick, and Michael Schoenhals. *Mao's Last Revolution.* Cambridge, MA: Belknap Press of Harvard University Press, 2008.

Márquez, Xavier. "Two Models of Political Leader Cults: Propaganda and Ritual." *Politics, Religion & Ideology* 19, no. 3 (2018): 268.

Martin, Peter. *China's Civilian Army: The Making of Wolf Warrior Diplomacy.* New York: Oxford University Press, 2021.

McElveen, Ryan. "Debunking Misconceptions About Xi Jinping's Anticorruption Campaign." *China-US Focus.* July 17, 2014.

McGregor, Richard. "Party Man: Xi Jinping's Quest to Dominate China." *Foreign Policy.* August 14, 2019.

McGregor, Richard. *Xi Jinping: The Backlash.* Melbourne: Penguin Random House Books, 2019.

Minzner, Carl. *End of an Era: How China's Authoritarian Revival Is Undermining Its Rise.* New York: Oxford University Press, 2018.

Nathan, Andrew J. "The Puzzle of Authoritarian Legitimacy." *Journal of Democracy* 31, no. 1 (2020): 158–168.

Nathan, Andrew J. "Who Is Xi." *New York Review of Books.* May 12, 2016.

Naughton, Barry. "Deng Xiaoping: The Economist." *China Quarterly* 135 (1993): 491–514.

Ong, Lynette H., and Christian Goebel. "Social Unrest in China." In Kerry Brown (ed.). *China and the EU in Context*. London: Palgrave MacMillan, 2014.

Patapan, Haig, and Yi Wang. "The Hidden Ruler: Wang Huning and the Making of Contemporary China." *Journal of Contemporary China* 27, no. 109 (2018): 47–60. https://research-repository.griffith.edu.au/bitstream /handle/10072/348664/PatapanPUB3927. pdf;jsessionid=8ADAB846 37D28A4CA08F2EBE413B89D4?sequence=1.

Pei Minxin. "China's Rule of Fear." *Project Syndicate*. February 8, 2015. www .project-syndicate.org/commentary/china-fear-bureaucratic-paralysis-by -minxin-pei-2016-02.

Peng Xizhe. "Demographic Consequences of the Great Leap Forward in China's Provinces." *Population and Development Review* 13, no. 4 (1987): 649.

Perry, Elizabeth J. "Cultural Governance in Contemporary China: 'Re-orienting' Party Propaganda." *Harvard-Yenching Institute Working Papers*. https://dash.harvard.edu/handle/1/11386987.

Pye, Lucien. *Asian Power and Politics: The Cultural Dimensions of Authority*. Cambridge, MA: Belknap Press of Harvard University Press, 1985.

Qian, Nancy. "The Case for Chinese Foreign Aid." *Project Syndicate*. November 8, 2021.

Qian Gang. "領袖姓名傳播強度觀察" [An observation on the intensity of the transmission of leaders' names]. Radio Television Hong Kong. July 11, 2014. http://app3.rthk.hk/mediadigest/content.php?aid=1563.

Qin Hui. 传统十论 [On the traditional ten]. Oriental Press, 2014.

Rees, E. A. "Leader Cults: Varieties, Preconditions and Functions." In Balázs Apor, Jan C. Behrends, Polly Jones, and E. A. Rees (eds.). *The Leader Cult in Communist Dictatorships*. London: Palgrave Macmillan, 2004.

Rene, Helena K. *China's Sent-Down Generation: Public Administration and the Legacies of Mao's Rustication Program*. Washington DC: Georgetown University Press, 2013.

Richardson, John G. (ed.). *Handbook of Theory and Research for the Sociology of Education*. New York: Greenwood Press, 1986.

Ringen, Stein. *The Perfect Dictatorship: China in the 21st Century*. Hong Kong: Hong Kong University Press, 2016.

Ross, Robert S., and Jo Inge Bekkevold (eds.). *China in the Era of Xi Jinping: Domestic and Foreign Policy Challenges*. Washington, DC: Georgetown University Press, 2016.

Rozman, Gilbert (ed.). *China's Foreign Policy: Who Makes It, and How Is It Made?* New York: Palgrave Macmillan, 2012.

Rudolf, Jennifer, and Michael Szonyi (eds.). *The China Questions: Critical Insights into a Rising Power*. Cambridge, MA: Harvard University Press, 2018.

Sæbø, Sun Heidi. *Kina—den nye supermakten: Jakten på Xi Jinping og det moderne Kina* [China—the new superpower: the hunt for Xi Jinping and modern China]. Oslo: Kagge, 2019.

Shambaugh, David (ed.). *China and the World*. New York: Oxford University Press, 2020.

Shambaugh, David. *China's Future*. Cambridge, UK: Polity Press, 2016.

Shambaugh, David. *China's Leaders: From Mao to Now*. Cambridge, UK: Polity Press, 2021.

Shih, Victor. *Coalitions of the Weak: Elite Politics in China from Mao's Stratagem to the Rise of Xi*. Cambridge: Cambridge University Press, 2022.

Shum, Desmond. *Red Roulette: An Insider's Story of Wealth, Power, Corruption and Vengeance in Today's China*. New York: Scribner, 2021.

Silver, Laura. "China's International Image Remains Broadly Negative as Views of the U.S. Rebound." Pew Research Center. June 30, 2021.

Smith, Graeme, and Louisa Lim. "Xi Dada and Daddy: Power, the Party and the President." *Little Red Podcast*. November 2, 2020. https://omny .fm/shows/the-little-red-podcast/xi-dada-and-daddy-power-the-party -and-the-presiden.

Smith, Stephen N. "China's 'Major Country Diplomacy': Legitimation and Foreign Policy Change." *Foreign Policy Analysis* 17, no. 2 (2021). https:// academic.oup.comm/fpa/article-abstract/17/2/orab002/6139347.

Stenslie, Stig, and Marte Kjær Galtung. "The Arab Spring Seen from Beijing." *Internasjonal Politikk* 4 (2014): 452–466.

Stenslie, Stig, and Marte Kjær Galtung. *49 Myths About China*. Lanham, MD: Rowman & Littlefield, 2015.

Stoltenberg, Clyde D. "China's Special Economic Zones: Their Development and Prospects." *Asian Survey* 24, no. 6 (1984).

Su Guanhua: "When Push Comes to Nudge: A Chinese Digital Civilisation in-the-Making." *Media International Australia* 173, no. 1 (2019).

Sun Chaoyi. "习总书记排队点餐取餐全程自己来" [General Secretary Xi queued up, ordered food, paid and did everything himself]. *Zhongguo Gongchandang xinwen*. December 29, 2012. www.scmp.com/news/china /article/1392160/president-xi-buys-meal-beijing-bun-shop.

Sverdrup Thygeson, Bjørnar, and Stig Stenslie. "Beijingology 2.0: Bridging the 'Art' and 'Science' of China Watching in Xi Jinping's New Era." *International Journal of Intelligence and Counterintelligence*. July 18, 2022.

Svolik, Milan: *The Politics of Authoritarian Rule*. Cambridge: Cambridge University Press, 2012.

Tan Jun (ed.). "The Image Crisis of Government Officials in 2012." Renmin University. January 2013.

Tang Fen. "Xi Jinping's Quotes Replace the Ten Commandments in Churches." *Bitter Winter*. September 14, 2019.

Teiwes, Frederick C. "The Study of Elite Politics in PRC: Politics Inside the 'Black Box.'" In David S. G. Goodman (ed.). *Handbook of Politics of China*. Cheltenham, UK: Edward Elgar, 2015.

Thomas, Neil. "China Politics 2025: Stronger as China Goes." MacroPolo. October 26, 2020.

Thomas, Neil. "Eye on 2022 (Part 2): Rising Stars in Beijing." MacroPolo. February 16, 2021.

Thomas, Neil. "Members Only: Recruitment Trends in the Chinese Communist Party Members." MacroPolo. July 15, 2015.

Thomas, Neil. "Ties That Bind: Xi's People on the Politburo." MacroPolo. June 17, 2020.

Tiezzi, Shannon. "Zhou Yongkang's Greatest Crime." *The Diplomat*. April 21, 2015.

Tong Yanqi. "Morality, Benevolence, and Responsibility: Regime Legitimacy in China from Past to the Present." *Journal of Chinese Political Science* 16, no. 2 (2011): 141–159.

Tong Yanqi and Lei Shaohua (eds.). *Social Protest in Contemporary China, 2003–2010: Transitional Pains and Regime Legitimacy*. New York: Routledge, 2014.

Torigian, Joseph. "Historical Legacies and Leaders' Worldviews: Communist Party History and Xi's Learned (and Unlearned) Lessons." *China Perspectives*. June 2018. https://journals.openedition. org/chinaperspectives/7548.

Tunsjø, Øystein. *The Return of Bipolarity in World Politics*. New York: Columbia University Press, 2018.

Ueki, Chikako Kawakatsu. "Liberal Deterrence of China: Challenges in Achieving Japan's China Policy." In Takashi Inoguchi, G. John Ikenberry, and Yoichiro Sato (eds.). *The U.S.-Japan Security Alliance: Regional Multilateralism*. New York: Palgrave Macmillan, 2011.

Vogel, Ezra F. *Deng Xiaoping and the Transformation of China*. Cambridge: Belknap Press of Harvard University Press, 2011.

Wang, Earl. "How Will the EU Answer China's Turn Toward 'Xi Jinping Thought on Diplomacy'?" *The Diplomat*. July 30, 2020.

Wang Heyan. "总后副部长谷俊山被查已有两年" [Vice director of PLA's Logistics Department, Gu Junshan, has been under investigation for two years]. *Shishi Zhongxin*. January 15, 2014.

Wang Xin. "北京观察：习近平为谁打破'七上八下'" [Who has Xi crushed 'seven up, eight down' for?]. *Duowei Xinwen*. October 29, 2015. www .dwnews.com.

Wang Yong. "Believers Forced to Worship China's Only God—President Xi." Association for the Defense of Human Rights and Religious Freedom. December 7, 2019. https://en.adhrrf.org/believers-forced-to-worship -chinas-only-god-president-xi.html.

Wang Yuhua. "Can the Chinese Communist Party Learn from Chinese Emperors?" In Jennifer Rudolph and Michael Szonyi (eds.). *The China Questions: Critical Insights into a Rising Power*. Cambridge, MA: Harvard University Press, 2018.

Wasserstrom, Jeffrey. "Why Are There No Biographies of Xi Jinping?" *The Atlantic*. January 30, 2021.

Watts, Elleka. "Prostitution Is Key to Reducing Corruption in China." *The Diplomat*. August 22, 2013.

Weber, Max. "The Sociology of Charismatic Authority." In M. Weber, H. Gerth, and C. W. Mills (eds.). *From Max Weber: Essays in Sociology*. New York: Oxford University Press, 1946.

Weber, Max, H. Gerth, and C. W. Mills (eds.). *From Max Weber: Essays in Sociology*. New York: Oxford University Press, 1946.

Wong, Edward, and Mia Li. "Keeping Count: Corrupt Chinese Officials and Their Mistresses." *Sinosphere*. April 27, 2015.

"The World's Most Powerful Man: Xi Jinping Has More Clout Than Donald Trump: The World Should Be Wary." *The Economist*. October 14, 2017.

Wu Jing. *Wolf Warrior* (战狼), 2015; *Wolf Warrior* 2 (战狼 2), 2017.

Wyne, Ali, and Ryan Hass. "China's Diplomacy Is Limiting Its Own Ambition." *Foreign Policy*. June 9, 2021.

Xi Jinping. *The Governance of China*. 4 vols. Beijing: Foreign Language Press, 2014, 2017, 2020, and 2022.

Xin Li and Kjeld Erik Brødsgaard. "SOE Reform in China: Past, Present and Future." *Copenhagen Journal of Asian Studies* 31, no. 2, 2013: 54–78.

Yahuda, M. "Kremlinology and the Chinese Strategic Debate, 1965–66." *China Quarterly* 49 (1972): 33–36.

Yin Liangen and Terry Flew. "Xi Dada Loves Peng Mama—Digital Culture and the Return of Charismatic Authority in China." *Thesis Eleven* 144, no. 1 (2018): 80–99.

Yuan Nansheng. "资深外交官 袁南生：疫情改变世界秩序，防止发生战略误判" [Senior diplomat Yuan Nansheng: the pandemic changes the world order and prevents strategic mistakes]. 163.com. May 3, 2020. www.163.com/dy/article/FBNBCQGN0514C8IB.html.

Yue Huairang. "赵立坚出任外交部新闻司副司长" [Zhao Lijian appointed vice director of the Information Department of the Foreign Ministry]. *The Paper*. August 23, 2019. www.thepaper.cn/newsDetail_forward _4236108.

Zha Jianying. "China's Heart of Darkness: Prince Han Fei and Chairman Xi Jinping: Part I: The Dark Prince." *China Heritage*. July 14, 2020.

Zhang Shaoying and Derek McGhee. *China's Ethical Revolution and Regaining Legitimacy: Reforming the Communist Party Through Its Public Servants*. Cham, Switzerland: Palgrave Macmillan, 2017.

Zhao Suisheng. "Foreign Policy Implications of Chinese Nationalism Revisited: The Strident Turn." *Journal of Contemporary China* 22, no. 82 (2013): 535–553.

Zheng Wang. "The Chinese Dream: Concept and Context." *Journal of Chinese Political Science* 19 (2013).

Zheng Wang. "The Next Hu." Wilson Center. December 20, 2012.

# Index

# About the Book

WITH STEELY DETERMINATION, XI JINPING HAS FORGED HIS WAY TO absolute power at home, consolidated China's role as a global superpower, and promoted instrumental myths about his life. All the while, in many ways he has remained a mystery. Which is a problem, assert Stig Stenslie and Marte Kjær Galtung, because to understand China today, it is essential to understand Xi.

Who is he? What is his vision for China? What explains his rise? How is he perceived by the masses? These are among the questions that gave rise to this book. Using Xi as a lens with which to examine China's political development over the past decade, the authors succeed in shining new light on the innermost circles of Chinese politics and on the authoritarian leader himself.

**Stig Stenslie** is research director and head of the Centre for Intelligence Studies at the Norwegian Intelligence School (NORIS). **Marte Kjær Galtung** is head teacher of Chinese and China studies at NORIS.